The
Public Sector Manager

Second Edition

Essential skills for
The public sector

Jennifer Bean
Lascelles Hussey

HB PUBLICATIONS
(Incorporated as Givegood Limited)

Published by:

HB Publications
London, England

First Published 2000 © HB Publications
Second Edition 2011 © HB Publications

British Library Cataloguing in Publication Data

ISBN 978 1 899448 92 0

For further information see www.hbpublications.com
and www.fci-system.com

Contents

Chapter 1

Introduction

The public sector is very diverse, and delivers a wide range of services. It often has to cope with a fast changing environment, brought about by changing public demand and new "political" directions. It also has to operate within financial and statutory constraints. In order to meet these challenges public sector managers need the same diverse range of skills required by the best private sector managers. In some areas of the public sector, managers even need to display "entrepreneurship".

The Public Sector Manager is a text that considers all the areas of skill and knowledge that a manager should possess in order to operate in today's public sector environment. Those already operating in the environment will recognise that managers cannot rely solely on the expertise in their chosen field or profession, and many other disciplines such as finance, marketing and human resource management are now required.

There are already many management books in the market place focusing on different aspects of management, covering the private and other sectors. Although management skills are often easily transferable across sectors, this book is different insofar as it is targeted specifically at public sector managers. It shows how the standard management techniques can be applied to the special experience managers will have of managing in public sector environments, along with the constraints that may bring. It is an ideal book for those already practicing as managers, those seeking to become managers, and those undertaking management qualifications.

The book begins with assisting the reader to identify their current position with respect to their management skills, and sets out the range and level of skills they should have in order to be an effective manager. Another key area covered is customer focus, which is now essential for all public sector organisations. It is good practice to ensure the services delivered are meeting the needs of the local community.

Other chapters consider general management techniques including managing resources and developing quality services, supply and demand, and the attributes of a public sector entrepreneur. All chapters have illustrative examples and practical ideas and exercises, which can be used for self-development or as a team event.

This book is one of a series of "Essential Skills for the Public Sector" titles. The series aims to assist public sector managers become more efficient and effective in carrying out their important management responsibilities. We consider this book to be an important part of the tool kit for public sector management development.

Chapter 2

The Public Sector Manager's Skill Base

To manage is defined in several ways, "to organise, regulate, be in charge of an organisation, team, etc.; to succeed in achieving; to meet one's needs with limited resources" (*The Concise Oxford Dictionary*)

A manager's role is to manage and deliver all of the above. Public sector managers require the same qualities, skills and knowledge as managers in any other sector. Although there are differences in the environments and the challenges that present themselves, the standard requirements for good management are equally applicable in the public sector as in any other sector.

The ideal attributes required of a public sector manager can be summarised in the following table:

Knowledge	Skill and Abilities	Personal Qualities
• Relevant information	• Decision making	• General attitude
	• Leadership	• Work ethic
• Service/Product technicalities	• Presentation	• Emotional control
• Professional Codes and Ethics	• Communication	• Self awareness
	• Motivation	• Pro-activity
• Corporate structures	• Negotiation	• Innovation

Knowledge	Skill and Abilities	Personal Qualities
▪ Policies and Procedures ▪ Corporate and Business Planning ▪ Finance ▪ Quality ▪ Marketing ▪ Personnel management ▪ Legislation	▪ Delegation ▪ Analytical (Problem solving) ▪ Lobbying	▪ Mental agility ▪ Vision

Most of the attributes can be learnt and developed over time, except for personal qualities, which tend to be inherent but can be modified with training. The learning process can be achieved through training, self-development, experimentation, reading, discovery and other management development techniques such as mentoring. The above attributes are discussed in the following paragraphs.

Knowledge

All jobs require a certain amount of knowledge which can be gathered through training, experience, discovery, practice, interactions, and so on. We gain additional knowledge about things on a daily basis and this is fundamental to being an effective manager.

Relevant Information

A manager is expected to know all the important information relevant to the service being managed.

Important information is difficult to define but would include information about how the service is delivered, such as the organisational structure, reporting lines, the target customer/user groups and so on. A good manager should gain as much information about the service as they can reasonably retain or alternatively, ensure important facts are stored in an easily retrievable format for when needed.

Service/Product technicalities

A manager is not expected to be a technician but should be aware of the technical details necessary to produce the service or product under management. For example, a manager responsible for the delivery of trading standards should understand the technical issues relating to weights and measures, similarly a school head teacher should know the technicalities of class control and the National Curriculum. Many services will have a <u>quality</u> or <u>procedure</u> manual which will set out details of the service and the practicalities of how it should be delivered, along with the quality standards that need to be achieved. Such manuals will aide the manager in learning the relevant information and service technicalities.

Professional Codes and Ethics

Professional knowledge is easily defined for service areas that require the attainment of professional examinations, or memberships of professional bodies. A manager who has a profession is assumed to be a "professional". This assumption comes from the fact that most professions have a code of conduct along with ethical guidelines regulated by the profession. Public sector managers are professionals in a wide range of activities including, teaching, accountancy, medicine, nursing, social work, planning, engineering, and so on.

Corporate structures

Every manager should have an understanding of the corporate structure of which they are a part. Most corporate structures are hierarchical in nature with a "chain of command". Knowing the reporting lines is essential for effective management. Structures can vary quite dramatically within the public sector with services being headed by elected members, boards of trustees, management boards, government appointees, boards of directors and so on. Some of the structures are very centralised and others very de-centralised, and therefore the manager role varies significantly with respect to the level of authority, decision making, accountability and responsibility. It is essential for a manager to be aware of the roles and responsibilities attached to their position and the part they will play in the organisation's overall management.

Policies and Procedures

Every organisation will have policies and procedures that all staff are expected to adhere to. They are usually in a written format and are often accessible on the organisation's intranet. They should at least be referred to as part of staff induction, particularly for a new manager. Policy and procedure documents will usually cover areas such as health and safety, equal opportunities, customer care, complaints, finance, and so on. Often there are so many policies and procedures that a manager cannot be expected to know all of them in detail, however, they should be aware of the range of areas covered, such that when policy or procedural issues arise, the appropriate manual can be referred to for guidance.

Corporate and Business Plans

Managers should be aware of the following:

The Vision and/or Mission Statements

A view of what the future organisation should be, as set out by the most senior decision makers responsible for directing the organisation

---

One or both of these should be found in the corporate plan, if the organisation has one. The corporate plan sets out the overall aims and objectives to be achieved and the broad strategies to be implemented. It should be the framework for all other plans developed by the organisation.

A manager should be involved in the planning process, at least at a local level for their area of service. This should result in a service or business plan setting out the short term objectives and the action plan required to achieve them.

Finance

Many managers may have undergone professional training and be well qualified in their field, however, given the emphasis on value for money, a knowledge of finance is

now important to every public sector manager. Finance may not have been a topic covered in a manager's prior training, but increasingly managers will be required to know about budgets, and will often be given budgetary responsibility. For example, local authorities often devolve budgets down to front line managers who should have knowledge of budget setting, monitoring, management and control. Knowledge can be gained through formal and on the job training, as well as through experiential learning.

Quality

Managers should be able to define what quality means for the service under their control. Once identified, the quality definition should be supported by standards that can be measured and monitored. Setting quality standards that are meaningful to the service providers and users is a skill in itself, and there are techniques that can be learned to assist in this area. A manager's understanding of quality is critical to achieving value for money and maximising the use of resources when delivering services.

Marketing

Marketing is not just for the marketing experts, and although managers may work in an organisation that has a marketing department, a professional manager needs to understand marketing in relation to the way in which services are delivered and perceived. In any organisation, every member of staff takes part in marketing. The way the telephone is answered, how people are greeted at reception, the style and content of letters and reports, all go to reflect the organisation's image and the way it is viewed. Managers need to have a basic knowledge of the critical inter-relationships between:

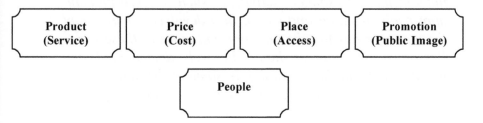

The top line is commonly referred to as the 4P's of marketing, and "People" sometimes the 5th P. Knowing who the people are with respect to a particular market place is critical. The public sector often has a very complex market place where "People" consist not just of "customers" but include:

- *Service purchasers*
- *Service users*
- *Partners*
- *Contractors*
- *Stakeholders*
- *The general public*

Managers need to understand research techniques, analysis of data, the product/customer mix, and so on, in order to develop effective marketing strategies and a truly "customer focussed" service.

Personnel Management

One of the keys to good management is the ability to get the most from staff, and managing staffing resources is often a major part of the management role. In numerous public sector organisations, a manager will have the support of a personnel department that will assist with many of the fundamental personnel activities, such as recruitment, appraisals, training and so on. In a devolved environment the manager has to take on more and more of these tasks. Personnel procedures should be well documented and managers should have training in some of the fundamental areas such as recruitment and selection, appraisal techniques, and equal opportunities. There are many facets to being proficient in the area of personnel management, ranging from motivating staff to managing absence. Some of these techniques can be learned, however many managers also need to work on their personal attributes in order to effectively manage an often diverse workforce.

Legislation

A manager should be aware of relevant legislation that affects all aspects of the working environment. This includes legislation relating to areas such as health and safety, consumer protection, contracts, employment and so on. Some areas of the public sector will be governed by specific legislation which controls their activities, setting standards, giving guidance etc. For example, there are a number of Local Government Acts, Housing Acts, Children's Acts, Police and Criminal Justice Acts, and so on. In addition to specific legislation, some areas of service will also need to be responsive to case law. This is especially important in areas such as medicine, where case law outcomes may have a significant impact on service delivery. The public sector tends to work in a regulatory and regulated environment, and as such a public sector manager has a duty of care to ensure that no legislation is knowingly breached.

Skills and Abilities

Skills and abilities are a practiced or expert way in which knowledge is used and applied. Ideally there should be continuous improvement in the delivery of the activity until an optimum or peak level is achieved. Skills may be manual, intellectual or social. A public sector manager should be skilled in most of the areas mentioned in the table on page 2, and have the ability to implement those skills. Depending on the nature of their position, and job role, a manager may not have the opportunity to practice certain skill areas, and hence will not be able to develop or improve them.

Decision Making

Decisions need to be made on a daily basis, but ideally they should be made with supporting knowledge and information which easily justifies the decision. There are a number of stages to the decision making process which are summarised as follows:

✓　*Be clear about the type of decision to be made:*

Objective decision based on facts
(Yes, go ahead with project A because we now have the funding)

Subjective decision based on facts and opinions
(Yes, go ahead with project A because I think we will be able to get the funding)

Comparative decision where a choice has to be made

(Yes, go ahead with project A instead of project B)

✓   *Have a good knowledge of all the relevant facts available underpinning the decision*

✓   *Where the facts are unknown or insufficient for objective decision making, draw on past experience and prior knowledge of similar situations. (If necessary consult with others who would have the knowledge and experience)*

✓   *Analyse how the decision will impact on achieving the service objectives*

✓   *Assess the level of risk attached to the decision*

✓   *Gather appropriate evidence to support the decision*

✓   *Ensure that the decision once made is properly implemented*

The ability to follow the above stages will vary depending on the timescales and urgency of the decision, and the relative impact the decision will have on the service, operations, staff, etc.

Leadership

Leadership is the ability to influence and direct others in a way that enables the group to achieve its goals. It is usual for managerial positions to be responsible for other staff. Hence, the manager usually has to be the leader of a team and therefore requires leadership skills. The management style adopted should reflect the size and nature of the team under the manager's control. An effective leader is able to adapt their leadership style to meet the needs of the team and achieve the service objectives.

Presentation

Presentation takes a number of formats including written, verbal, and visual, and as with most skills, practice makes perfect. Presentation skills are required by all managers as depending on their specific role, they will frequently have to present information to staff, clients, senior managers and the public. Personal attributes such as confidence and clarity assist in the effectiveness of presentations, but even without these attributes, presentations can be improved significantly. One approach is to have a very good underpinning knowledge of the subject being presented, and the nature of the audience. This enables the presentation to be pitched appropriately.

Communication

The results of many internal staff surveys regularly highlight the communication factor within the organisation. The criticism is usually of very poor top down communication, no channel for bottom up communication and very little peer group communication. Effective communication is an essential skill for all managers as it impacts on the way information is given and received. Managers need to be able to transmit information to senior management and staff using a number of different modes and means of communication. They also have to ensure they are receptive of messages being communicated by others. Ideally an organisation should have clear mechanisms in place for formal communication as well as opportunities for informal communication.

Motivation

The ability to motivate others is a skill which can be learned and developed through training and practice. There are a number of psychological theories relating to motivation including Maslow's hierarchy of needs, Herzberg's theory of motivation at work, and Vroom's expectancy theory to name three. We do not intend to cover these theories in this text, however, their common link is that individuals have needs that they wish to satisfy in some way, and that includes satisfaction at work. Understanding what motivates individuals is an important starting point for managers that have to motivate a staff team, and they should adopt a number of different approaches. Some of the key motivational factors are identified as follows:

Employees may have some of the following needs...		Areas of satisfaction may include...
A regular income	⮡	Pay rates, availability of paid overtime, terms and conditions of employment, permanent post, and so on
Job security	⮡	Terms and conditions of employment
Self esteem and recognition	⮡	Job titles, promotion prospects, pay rates, grades, awards and public recognition
Group membership	⮡	Group activities, friendly atmosphere, relations with others

Support and care	➲	Pay and benefits, attitude to sickness, family care policies, helpfulness
Self development	➲	Training policy, promotion prospects, learning opportunities
Routine	➲	Job consistency, management consistency, supervision
Conducive environment	➲	Attractive offices and furnishings, cleanliness, comfort
Regular challenges and interest	➲	Job variety, learning opportunities, promotion
Control and independence	➲	No interference, very little management, promotion, managing others

The areas of satisfaction may be used as motivators. However, a mixed group of staff may have differing needs, some of which may conflict, making the choice of motivators more difficult.

Public sector organisations may face difficulties in motivating staff where the key motivator is pay or promotion. Strict human resource policies often mean that pay rates are fixed according to scales regardless of merit, (e.g. bonuses are often not possible) and staff cannot be automatically promoted into higher graded positions. This leaves the public sector manager often struggling to find more innovative and creative ways to motivate staff. One approach used in some organisations is to allow more flexible working arrangements such as home working, job sharing, part-time hours and so on, allowing staff to balance home and work more easily.

Negotiation

Negotiation skills are needed by all public sector managers particularly those with budgetary and staffing responsibilities. Public sector managers will find themselves negotiating with:

- *Staff*
- *Contractors*
- *Suppliers of goods and services*
- *Unions*
- *Funders*
- *Partners – public, voluntary, and private sector*
- *Clients and customers*
- *Line and senior managers*
- *Other operational, support service and central departments*

Good negotiators will have set a goal and preferred outcome, which guides the negotiations from the outset. They should have also considered the impact of a range of potential outcomes, such that they know the effect of any compromises they may decide to make.

Delegation

There is always a conflict between delegation and control. If areas of control are delegated, the manager is immediately reliant on the ability of others to undertake the delegated tasks. This results in a certain element of control being lost. Sometimes the organisational culture will make managers very wary of losing control, as in the event of something going wrong the manager is still held to account, even though someone else may have been responsible. Delegation is important and knowing when and what to delegate is an essential element of good management.

Analytical (Problem solving)

The word analyse has arisen in several of the other skill areas and being able to analyse issues is an important skill area in its own right. A manager will require analytical skills to:

- *Interpret data*
- *React to problems*
- *Make decisions*
- *Understand change*
- *Gain knowledge*
- *Assess risk*
- *Provide solutions*
- *Set standards*
- *Monitor performance*

All the above is fundamental to problem solving which is a skill expected of managers. Problems often arise on a daily basis and the manager should be able to react quickly and provide the appropriate solutions. If problems are not dealt with promptly and remain unresolved, they could result in serious consequences for the organisation.

Lobbying

Lobbying is the practice of seeking to influence and solicit support from influential people. Who is seen as influential will vary depending on the organisation and the particular circumstances. For example, the influential person may be:

- *A senior manager*
- *A director, chief executive*
- *A board member, committee member, trustee*
- *A government department or individual within the department*
- *A politician or public official*

From time to time managers may have to lobby an influential person in order to progress service developments, gain more financial support, resist service closure, and so on. It is important for public sector managers to understand the lobbying protocol applicable to their particular organisation.

Personal Qualities

General Attitude

Attitudes reflect an individual's way of responding to objects, events and situations based on their prior experience, culture, and upbringing. The importance of attitudes varies depending on the type and nature of the job. If the role is a very structured or automated occupation, attitudes tend to be less important than in occupations that have a bias towards free will and self regulation, such as a management role. Attitudes tend to affect the following important issues:

- *Commitment*
- *Loyalty*

- *Consistency*
- *Responsibility*

The "right" attitude will vary considerably from organisation to organisation depending on the organisational culture. Moulding attitudes to suit the requirements of the organisation is very difficult and training is not always an effective solution. One approach is establishing an environment where peer pressure will encourage individual attitudes to conform to the organisational "norm".

Work Ethic

This often stems from the general attitude, and again the correct type of work ethic arises from the organisational culture. Problems emerge when the organisational culture produces a work ethic which is not desired by the organisation. For example, there may be a culture whereby all staff leave work at 5.00pm exactly, regardless of the status of their work, however, the organisation may prefer a work ethic whereby staff work until certain jobs are completed and timescales met. The growing trend in the public sector is to promote a hard working approach and image, which can flexibly meet the needs of service users. For example, weekend opening at doctor's surgeries, 24 hour help lines for many public services, and out of hours working expected from some types of staff.

Emotional Control

All staff should exercise emotional control within the work place. This is especially needed for public sector staff and managers who may face a number of challenges:

- *Becoming too involved with a client and their needs*

- *Growing emotionally attached to clients*

- *Having to make decisions which may make the difference between life and death*

- *Imparting good and bad news to clients and their families, and facing the response*

- *Working in areas of danger, deprivation, and hostility*

- *Trying to deliver services with insufficient resources*

Managers must remember that boundaries have to be drawn, and that they have a responsibility to staff and clients to maintain control over their feelings at all times. Managers must therefore be aware of how they feel at any given moment in time, and assess whether or not it is appropriate to have, or more importantly show, those feelings in a professional environment. This is part of being a professional!

Self awareness

As stated above, managers must be aware of themselves. This awareness should include:

- *Emotions and feelings*
- *Knowledge and skills*

- *How they communicate, upwards, downwards and laterally*
- *How they communicate with clients and the general public*
- *Body language*
- *Work ethic*
- *Reliability*
- *Habits*
- *Health*
- *Cultural conditioning and background*

Managers should consider their strengths and weaknesses in all the above areas, and be honest about their weaknesses such that they can take action to develop and improve those areas.

Pro-activity

Pro-active managers do not wait for things to happen and then react. They should be active in predicting what may happen in the future and taking action in advance. A pro-active manager, therefore, has more control over the service and resources under their control. Even if pro-activity is not a strong personal attribute, it can be improved by establishing systems that provide the information required to be pro-active. These include:

- *Regular reports on service activity, e.g. number of users, productivity statistics, and so on.*

- *Trend analysis and forecasting, e.g. establishing demand growth or decline, calculating growth rates, calculating future impact on the service*

- *Comparisons with other organisations e.g. what changes are being made with respect to the delivery of like for like services, are there differences in service quality, are other organisations experiencing the same demand changes and trends*

- *Market place information, analysis and monitoring, e.g. "what is the relationship between supply and demand in your market place, is the balance changing, are new providers entering the market place?"*

- *Regular financial information, monitoring present performance, forecasting future performance*

- *Value for money indicators such as unit costs*

Public sector managers sometimes find it difficult to be pro-active given the organisational and service constraints within which they have to work. However, showing pro-activity is now a very important attribute.

Innovation

Ideally, managers should be creative within the scope of their work and develop ideas and solutions that will improve the service and address weaknesses. The ability to be innovative will not be present in all managers. In such cases, managers should have sufficient self awareness to identify this as an area for which outside assistance may be required. In the private sector, it is quite common for research and development departments to be funded to create innovative ideas that can be tried and tested before being introduced for wider use. In the public sector there is often comparatively little funding for such departments, and it is the manager's responsibility to try and gain innovation from within their own service area. Innovations in the public sector can come from:

- *Staff*
- *Service users*
- *The general public*
- *Competitors*
- *Other service providers*
- *Other regions*
- *Central government*

Public sector managers need to encourage innovations that can lead to changes which benefit service quality and helps to achieve value for money.

Mental agility

This personal attribute is the ability to assimilate information quickly and respond appropriately. This is required when faced with questions that need to be answered on the spot, or when decisions need to be made immediately or under pressure. It is a particularly useful attribute to have in a fast changing environment, where the manager has to keep abreast of many new developments, and be flexible with respect to ensuring services are delivered in a way which meets new requirements. For example, the emergency services are confronted with unique problems on a daily basis and managers need to be able to respond accordingly.

Vision

Managers that have vision of where they want the organisation or service to be in the future, are usually those who drive forward change in order to realise that vision. Ideally a vision should be communicated and shared, but it usually takes special individuals to create the vision that others can see and sign up to.

Having read through the list of attributes, it should be emphasised that even good managers do not necessarily have all the attributes mentioned above, and there is always scope for management development in one or more of the areas. Ideally, a management team should strive to have a mix of managers that between them do have all of the knowledge, skills, and personal qualities mentioned above. Each can then compensate for the gaps that may be present in the other.

Summary

❑ *Public sector managers require knowledge, skill and a number of personal qualities which are expected in good managers. This books defines 28 attributes that public sector managers should seek to acquire or improve upon*

❑ *If managers are aware of areas of weakness or gaps in their range of knowledge and skill, they should seek to develop themselves through training, self-development aids, reading, or other management development activities such as mentoring.*

❑ *Managers can improve their skills through experience and on the job practice.*

❑ *The management team should ideally include a mix of individuals with differing strengths such that all the attributes for successful management are apparent in one or more of the team members.*

Exercise 1

What attributes are most important?

You are a relatively new manager and are part of a recruitment panel that is trying to select a manager, who will be joining your team and will be working closely with you in order to deliver services. You have a clear vision and are keen and enthusiastic about the opportunities for change, development, improvement and innovation that exist for the service. Although you are new to this service area, you have already been complimented on your excellent management skills and abilities. You hope that any new incumbent would compliment your managerial attributes. After a rigorous recruitment process, based on an assessment of three key areas as identified in "The Public Sector Manager", three candidates emerged with equal scores, but distributed across different areas as follows:

	Candidate A	Candidate B	Candidate C
Knowledge	20	45	35
Skills and abilities	35	20	45
Personal qualities	45	35	20
Total	100	100	100

Each area was scored out of a total of 50.

Each member of the recruitment team is asked to present their preferred candidate based on the above results, and state clearly why they consider that candidate would be the best manager for the service.

Identify which candidate you would select: **A   B   C**

Set out and justify the reasons for your choice

Would your choice be different if selecting a candidate for the Chief Executive position?

A suggested solution can be found on page 138

Exercise 2

What is your skill base?

Self Assessment

For each of the 28 attributes listed below, score yourself between 1 and 10, where 1 represents a weakness and 10 a strength. Justify your score by giving a reason.

Attribute	Score 1 - 10	Reason for score
Knowledge		
Relevant information		
Service/Product technicalities		
Professional Codes and Ethics		
Corporate structures		
Policies and Procedures		
Corporate and Business Planning		
Finance		
Quality		
Marketing		

Attribute	Score 1 - 10	Reason for score
Personnel management		
Legislation		
Skills and Abilities		
Decision making		
Leadership		
Presentation		
Communication		
Motivation		
Negotiation		
Delegation		
Analytical (Problem solving)		
Lobbying		
Personal Qualities		
General attitude		
Work ethic		
Emotional control		

Attribute	Score 1 - 10	Reason for score
Self awareness		
Pro-activity		
Innovation		
Mental agility		
Vision		

For answer guide see page 139

Exercise 3

Is your manager a good public sector manager?

Upward Assessment

For each of the 28 attributes listed below, score your manager between 1 and 10 where 1 represents a weakness and 10 a strength. Justify your score by giving a reason.

Attribute	*Score 1 - 10*	*Reason for score*
Knowledge		
Relevant information		
Service/Product technicalities		
Professional Codes and Ethics		
Corporate structures		
Policies and Procedures		
Corporate and Business Planning		
Finance		
Quality		
Marketing		

Attribute	Score 1 - 10	Reason for score
Personnel management		
Legislation		
Skills and Abilities		
Decision making		
Leadership		
Presentation		
Communication		
Motivation		
Negotiation		
Delegation		
Analytical (Problem solving)		
Lobbying		
Personal Qualities		
General attitude		
Work ethic		
Emotional control		
Self awareness		
Pro-activity		

Attribute	Score 1 - 10	Reason for score
Innovation		
Mental agility		
Vision		

For answer guide see page 141

Exercise 4

Training Solutions

a) Having undertaken exercise 2 and 3, are there any areas of weakness that need to be addressed for you or your manager? If so, list them below and try and identify how those issues can be addressed either through training or some other form of management or personal development.

	Areas of weakness	*Training and development solutions*
Yourself		
Your manager		

Chapter 3

Developing a Customer Focus

Public sector managers are in the business of delivering services to customers. Therefore, they should be customer focussed which means putting the customer first, ensuring the service is geared to the customer wants and needs rather than being "an end in itself". This may result in the service having to be reassessed in order to meet any changes in customer requirements. This approach has always been adopted by those private sector organisations which depend on customers for their livelihood, and cannot afford to ignore changes in customer preferences.

Often the customer relationship is not clear cut in the public sector. It is complicated by the fact that there may be more than one customer to satisfy and other factors may affect the ability to change the service, such as legislation.

Who are the Customers?

For many public sector organisations there may be a variety customers which will usually fit into one or more of the following categories:

A Purchaser

This is the type of customer which is most closely aligned to the private sector. The purchaser may be an individual purchasing a membership to a publicly run leisure centre or purchasing a private bedspace in a public hospital, or it may be an organisation purchasing services on behalf of a group of people, such as a voluntary organisation hiring a room in a school or community centre. In all case a direct payment is made to the organisation for goods and services being provided.

A User

This is perhaps the most common type of customer for the public sector, and is usually a member of the general public. Services such as hospitals, schools, libraries, etc. are used mainly free of direct charges, and so the normal private sector customer relationship with the organisation is different. The user is not as powerful a customer as a purchaser because they do not make direct payments, and therefore cannot necessarily have a direct impact on whether or not the service continues to exist. This gives the supplier more control over what type of service is delivered. However, users do pay for public services indirectly through local and national taxes. They can ultimately have an impact on service suppliers by influencing key decision makers, such as politicians, councillors etc., although this may take time.

A Commissioner

This may be another public authority responsible for commissioning services and with control of financial resources. Whereas the purchaser would tend to select from the range of services currently on offer, a commissioner is likely to invest in developing a new service or making major changes to an existing service. Commissioners will tend to make large scale purchases and are therefore very important from the service provider's viewpoint.

The General Public

Unlike a specific user of service such as an older person using meals on wheels, the wider general public is also a customer irrespective of the local area in which they live. The public use services across the country such as the roads, emergency services, and so on.

Other Interested Parties

There may be other stakeholders who could be perceived as customers such as, other partners from the public and private sectors, central government departments, service inspectorates, government quangos, elected officials, and so on. These customers usually require information and often their views will have a direct impact on the way in which services are delivered.

Given the above, a public sector manager may have a very wide range of customers to focus on, some of whom will have conflicting wants and needs. For example, local residents may want parking restrictions on their residential streets, whereas the general public would wish to park on them without having to pay parking penalties, particularly if they happen to be near shopping centres or train networks.

The Importance of Customer Focus in the Public Sector

Usually a public sector organisation is funded mainly with public money to provide services. Hence, the emphasis has been placed on maximising service delivery within the available financial constraints. In the private sector, there is no service without the customer. If the customer does not buy, the service eventually has to cease. This only holds true for public services which rely mainly on income from purchasers. Other services are financed through tax revenues, and delivered even when some customers do not even want them, such as enforcement and control type services. For example, the public prosecution service is welcomed by the general public, but not desired by the criminals.

Customer focus is important in the public sector because:

❖ *Customer satisfaction saves money*

❖ *Reduced customer complaints save money*

❖ *Failure to meet certain customer's needs can result in legal action, costs and compensation*

❖ *Targets, benchmarks and performance indicators with respect to customers have to be met*

❖ *Achieving value for money services requires customer involvement*

❖ *The best ideas for service improvements are most likely to come from customers*

❖ *Service priorities should reflect customer needs*

❖ *In some cases, the customer can choose alternative service providers, and a reduction in demand for a service may make it unviable*

❖ *The views of customers affect the organisation's public image*

The benefits of customer focus are illustrated below.

A local authority decided to establish a number of One-Stop Shops throughout the local area as a way of becoming more customer focused. They were designed to handle the vast majority of customer enquiries, and included cashiers services such that customers could also pay rent, council tax, and other bills as part of their visit. Users were surveyed with a view to establishing levels of customer satisfaction and to identify improvements that could be made. Staff considered the number of users was already too high leading to high waiting times, and were not keen to encourage a further growth in demand. Although the organisation had thought the service was very customer focussed, the survey showed high levels of dissatisfaction. The points mentioned included:

■ Slow response times

■ Poor toilet facilities

■ No children's facilities

■ Few and uncomfortable seats in the waiting area

■ No access to drinks whilst waiting

■ Lack of privacy when speaking to staff

■ Poorly trained staff

■ No internet access points

Suggestions for improvement included:

■ More seating for waiting areas

- A crèche or soft play area for children

- A number of terminals which could access the authority's website such that visitors could gain information on-line without waiting to see a staff member

- A vending machine for hot and cold drinks

- Forms, such as planning applications, permit applications etc. out on display eliminating the need to queue and request them

- A waiting time display

- Staff development to make them more knowledgeable, friendly and responsive to customers

The survey also asked customers what, if anything, they would be prepared to pay for. Surprisingly most people were prepared to pay small amounts for certain services, such as use of the children's play area, food and drink, and certain information booklets.

The survey information resulted in a number of changes as most of the areas of dissatisfaction were dealt with and the suggestions implemented. The overall effect was to:

- reduce waiting times by 50% as customers were able to help themselves to information more easily via the computer or by accessing the relevant forms

- reduce the need for as many staff as those in post were more highly trained and efficient

- increase satisfaction levels of customers and reduce complaints

- change the atmosphere within the One-Stop Shop site as people were no longer as disgruntled by long and uncomfortable waiting conditions

- generate a small amount of income through the introduction of charges for certain services, the collection of which was easily achieved via the cashiers on site, and vending machine profits

Overall there was a net saving achieved and an improved service.

Changing the Relationship Between Management and Customers

The following diagram shows the common triangular relationship between management and customers and how that triangle should be reversed.

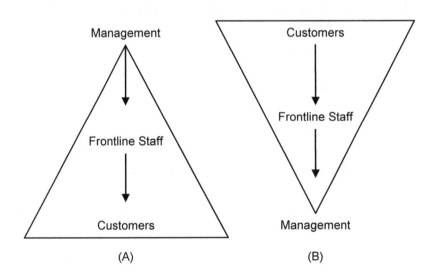

The most traditional model is shown by triangle (A), where management is at the apex with a top down management style setting out the tasks to be achieved by staff. The frontline staff

then have the interface with the customer, or service user, whose views are sometimes not taken into account.

Triangle (B) shows the customers at the top communicating their wants, needs and ideas to frontline staff who through a bottom up process of communication, are able to feed this information to management. With this information management can then determine the services and the appropriate allocation of resources. Having the customer driving the service, its content, and how it is delivered enables the organisation to become more customer focussed.

Some managers may consider that triangle B is not appropriate depending on the type of service being delivered. In some sectors customers do not know what they need, (e.g. doctor/ patient relationship), or do not want what they are being provided with (e.g. certain social services client interventions or parking enforcement).

Even in such cases a customer focus should not be lost. The customer may have limited influence over the content of the service, but can still be involved in how the service is delivered within any existing legal constraints. For example, customers' views should be taken into account when deciding service delivery aspects such as:

❖ *Location of the service (central, local, high street, mobile, combined services)*

❖ *Accessibility (opening hours, style of literature, information points, transportation)*

❖ *Levels of staffing (response times, face to face contact)*

❖ *Use of information technology (on-line information, availability of terminals)*

❖ *Methods of payment (direct debit, credit cards, credit arrangements, cash)*

❖ *Communication methods (telephone, post, on-line, languages)*

❖ *Communication style (caring, friendly, helpful)*

In order to achieve a triangle B approach, the public sector manager needs to become truly customer focussed. The attributes of a customer focussed manager is described in the following section.

Attributes of a Customer Focussed Manager

A customer focussed manager.....

❖ *Is knowledgeable about the customers (however they are defined)*

❖ *Fosters good customer relations*

❖ *Communicates with customers on a regular basis*

❖ *Establishes customer needs and wants*

❖ *Ensures the service is accessible and easy to understand*

❖ *Ensures a high level of customer satisfaction is achieved at all times (targets should be set)*

❖ *Changes the service to meet customer needs*

❖ *Responds quickly and efficiently to complaints*

Knowing the Customer

The first step to really knowing the customer is identifying <u>*who is*</u> *the customer. The manager must establish what defines the customer, and if there are more than one type of customer, determine which customer preference takes precedence. For example, a social services residential home will have two types of customers, the elderly person who is the user of service, and the purchaser of the bedspace who may be an in-house commissioner/social worker, or a relative. In some cases the user and purchaser may be the same. This service should consider both parties as customers and should seek to know everything about them.*

The second step is to determine what one needs to know about the customer, and then identify how that information can be obtained. A customer focussed manager should try to identify as much as possible about the customers' wants, needs, expectations, opinions, and ideas. In some cases service preferences and financial position are also relevant. This information can be gained from a range of sources:

- *Application forms*
- *Monitoring forms*
- *Case files*
- *Service history*
- *Interviews*
- *Questionnaires*

- *Meetings*
- *Discussion groups and forums*

In order to use the information, it needs to be collated in an easily retrievable format. This can be achieved by developing a customer database (very common in the private sector). Legislation regarding data protection, ethical codes of conduct, and privacy laws should be observed at all times.

This knowledge of the customer can be used to target services more effectively and assists in ensuring customer satisfaction is maximised.

Fostering Good Customer Relations

Good customer relations can yield many tangible and intangible benefits. For example, using the same residential home setting, if the home has good relations with its users they will have greater satisfaction levels. They will be more likely to want to stay in the home and they will act as advocates by recommending the home to others. Good relations with the purchasers will mean they are more likely to accept price increases, to make donations when needed, and will also make recommendations to others.

In order to build a relationship with the customer, the service has to attract their attention. Many public services go unnoticed until there is a problem. Ideally the manager should ensure customers are aware of the service before a problem occurs. It is at this point that good customer relations can be developed. It is more difficult to achieve good customer relations when the customer is already disgruntled and complaining about the service.

Some important issues for fostering good customer relations are summarised as follows:

- *Treat every customer as an individual without bias or discrimination of any kind*

- *Ensure that the customer feels valued and important*

- *Gain an understanding of customer expectations even if they are unrealistic*

- *Educate the customer about the service and the constraints (if any)*

- *Empathise with customer's problems and difficulties, and solve them where possible*

- *Enter into regular communication with the customer (see below)*

- *React positively to complaints (see last paragraph of this chapter)*

- *Ensure staff are trained in the delivery of all of the above*

Regular Communication with Customers

This is the cornerstone of being customer focussed. Many managers may consider the problem with the theory is the practice. It is very time consuming to engage in regular communication with customers and often time is not available. A lot depends on the method of communication adopted and the systems in place. Communication methods include:

- *Telephone, or on-line surveys and questionnaires*
- *Meetings*
- *Interviews*
- *Focus groups*
- *Random follow up calls*
- *E-mails*
- *Newspaper articles*
- *Newsletters*
- *Feedback sheets*
- *Annual reports*
- *Brochures*
- *Messaging via text, or networking websites*

If a variety of methods are chosen, the communication can be regular but not perceived as boring or repetitive. Effective communication is the best way to foster good customer relations. It also allows customers to put forward ideas for service development and to become involved with the service provision. The communication formats used should take into account language differences, disabilities, and cultural diversity.

Establishing Customer Needs and Wants

Often needs and wants are different. The service provider will tend to concentrate on assessing and delivering what the customer needs, whereas the customer is more concerned with their wants and hence the difference between the two often causes dis-satisfaction. Understanding the customers' wants and needs assists the manager to reduce dissatisfaction. For example:

Customer Needs	Customer Wants	Difference	Solution
Older person needs care in a residential setting	To stay in own home with pet	Location and care of animals	Educating the customer to understand the needs. Keeping customer in same locality, <u>ideally</u> satisfying the want of keeping the pet. (although this may be unlikely)
A regular refuse collection service	To be able to choose which day refuse is collected	Timing of collections	Ensuring some type of consultation has been undertaken with customers about the timing of collections and using the majority view for setting the timetable within practical constraints. Making public the results of such consultation and how the decision was arrived at.

Customer Needs	Customer Wants	Difference	Solution
Emergency temporary accommodation in what ever area is available	Permanent accommodation in an area of choice	Service availability and location	Educating the customer with respect to available services given their position. Informing the customer that in the longer term their wants will be considered and met within the existing constraints and criteria.

In the public sector many of the choices made and the solutions on offer are restricted by cost. In some cases, customers may be prepared to pay extra in order to satisfy their wants. The manager may be aware of this if good customer relations have been developed. Educating the customer is also critical in bringing wants and needs closer together.

Ensuring Service Accessibility
If customers are important, they need to be able to access services easily. This means:

✓ *They must know that the service exists and their eligibility, (service must be promoted)*

✓ *They must be able to understand the information provided about the service, (it must be in languages and formats that can be understood, including plain English)*

✓ *They must be able to physically obtain the service, (transportation, location, customer friendly buildings including disabled access etc.)*

For example, a youth club is based and situated in a portakabin in the middle of a primary school play area. Very few young people knew of its existence as it was not visible from the street, and there were no signs indicating it was there. There was no individual publicity for the site (although it was mentioned in a general brochure listing all the youth clubs) explaining the available activities, opening hours and so on. Due to the low numbers of users, it was eventually earmarked for closure.

Clearly, such examples show wasted resources and a loss of what might have been a very important service benefiting many potential users. The intangible costs of closure may be increased vandalism, youth crime, etc. as there are no longer services in the area for that group.

Achieving High Levels of Customer Satisfaction

A high level of customer satisfaction is an indicator that the service is meeting customer needs and even their wants as well. It is an important measure of how well the service is being delivered or certainly perceived. Targets should be set for levels of customer satisfaction and ratings should be obtained on a regular basis, at least annually.

If high levels of satisfaction are not being achieved, a customer focussed manager should be finding out why, and then taking appropriate action to improve the ratings. Even with services where the customer may incur a financial penalty, or have to be told that they cannot obtain what they want, satisfaction can still be assessed by asking customers about the process, its clarity, its fairness and so on.

Some public services have regular inspections by regulatory bodies that report on standards of service, and provide recommendations for improvement. In some instances where poor service standards are identified, inspectors may suggest changes to the management team, suspending funding, or even closure.

Changing the Service to Meet Customer Needs

In addition to knowing the customers, a manager should also keep abreast of the market place and the changes that are taking place within it. Customer needs will generally change over time as the market and society evolves. For example, many people are now paying bills such as council tax, using credit cards, direct debits and bank transfers over the internet rather than by cash or cheque. Services need to respond to changing customer requirements by providing systems that allow customers to pay in the way they wish.

It is not always possible for public services to respond quickly to changing customer needs and there may be a significant time lag before the service changes. However, the organisation and its management should always show a willingness to change and develop a strategy that allows change to occur. Failure to respond to change may result in services being outsourced to third parties who are more flexible in their approach.

Responding Quickly and Efficiently to Complaints

In the private sector a complaint is often viewed in a positive manner because:

- ✓ *It informs the business of what it is doing wrong and how it can be improved*

- ✓ *It gives the business the opportunity to rectify the problem for the customer*

- ✓ *It enables the business manager to turn a dis-satisfied customer into a very satisfied one, as they see the complaint being dealt with efficiently with a positive outcome*

- ✓ *It hopefully retains the customer for future business as opposed to losing a customer. Often people who do not complain demonstrate their dis-satisfaction by not making any future purchases*

The same approach can be taken in the public sector, however, it is not always possible to turn a dis-satisfied customer into a satisfied one, especially when the dissatisfaction is with a policy or a piece of legislation which is outside of the manager's control and cannot be changed. For example, a customer submitting a planning application which falls outside of building regulations will have the plans rejected, and may be dissatisfied as a result. The manager cannot change the regulations to satisfy the customer in this case, however the service could provide advice on how the application could be amended to meet the regulations, hence alleviating at least some of the dissatisfaction.

Summary

❑ *A public sector manager needs to be customer focussed which means putting the customer as the top priority when developing and delivering services*

❑ *In the public sector the customer may take a number of different forms. The public sector manager needs to understand who the customers are, and have some idea of the priority between different types of customer*

❑ *Being customer focussed and fostering good customer relations has tangible benefits that can result in savings, more efficient services and higher levels of customer satisfaction*

❑ *A customer focussed manager really knows the customers wants and needs and seeks to satisfy them within the available constraints*

❑ *Often customers need to be educated as to what the realistic expectations should be with respect to public services. This can only be achieved by effective and regular communication with customers*

Exercise 5

Developing a Customer Focus

Jason Coningsby (JC), senior manager of a prison, has been told to become more customer focussed as a result of a monitoring review by the local Prisoners Support Association (PSA). The PSA report sets out a wide range of complaints by inmates including:

- *Poor physical conditions (broken showers, blocked toilets, etc.)*
- *Lack of activities*
- *Lack of equipment and facilities*
- *Limited range and content of meals*
- *Overcrowding*
- *No educational programme*
- *Little communication from management with frontline staff*
- *Under qualified staffing and very little staff training*
- *No forum for communicating with staff or management*
- *Very little pastoral care*

Many more points were made and the report tried to relate the lack of customer focus to the recent spate of suicides and suicide attempts that have recently occurred. The prison has received a great deal of very bad publicity during the year, as in addition to the suicides mentioned, there has been two successful breaches of security leading to escapes. Although the prisoners were eventually recaptured, there has been significant concern over the management of the prison and the PSA report has been a final blow.

JC has been given 6 months by the governing body to develop an overarching action plan that will totally change the way in which the service is currently managed. A failure to produce something of substance may result in the prison being managed by another organisation. A key part of that action plan is the development of a customer focussed approach to service delivery.

JC was unclear as to how customer focus could be achieved in a prison, given that the inmates were certainly not willing customers, and the real customer was the Government who were paying for the facility. In order to assist him in meeting his target he decided to engage a consultant.

As a consultant, develop a list of practical actions that JC could take in order to develop a more customer focussed management approach.

Short Term Actions	Longer Term Actions

Short Term Actions	Longer Term Actions

For a suggested solution see page 142

Exercise 6

What is your customer definition?

a) Define who your customers are within each category. (Note, not all categories will be applicable and some customers may be included in more than one category)

Purchasers e.g. Fee paying parents and the local authority	**Users** e.g. Children and parents
Commissioner e.g. Health authority for special disability project	**General Public** e.g. Local residents, particularly potential users

Examples given are for a children's nursery

b) List below the ways in which you communicate with each of the above customer groups

Customer/Purchaser	Communication Method
Purchaser	
User	
Commissioner	
General Public	

Exercise 7

How well do you know your customers?

List 10 things that you know about your customers

1	⇨	*e.g. name, address, reason for contact, age, service history, etc.*

2	⇨	

3	⇨	

4	⇨	

5	⇨	

6	⇨	

7	⇨	

8	⇨	

9   ⇨

10   ⇨

List 10 things that you ought to know about your customers and how you can find out

	What I should know?	How can I find out?
1 ⇨	*e.g. are they happy with the service?*	*e.g. response to satisfaction questionnaire*
2 ⇨		
3 ⇨		
4 ⇨		
5 ⇨		
6 ⇨		
7 ⇨		
8 ⇨		

9 ⇨	
10 ⇨	

Exercise 8

Continuous Improvement

You may already consider that you have a good customer focus (or not!), but there is always scope for improvement. Using the following checklist, identify how you could improve in each of the areas, and indicate whether such improvements can be achieved immediately, in the short term (within a year) or in the long term (more than a year).

Customer Focus	Scope for Improvement	Now (✓)	Short Term (✓)	Long Term (✓)
Knowing customer details		☐	☐	☐
Fostering customer relations		☐	☐	☐
Regular customer communication		☐	☐	☐
Knowing customer needs and wants		☐	☐	☐
Service accessibility		☐	☐	☐
Level of customer satisfaction		☐	☐	☐

Customer Focus	Scope for Improvement	Now (✓)	Short Term (✓)	Long Term (✓)
Service flexibility and change		☐	☐	☐
Responsiveness to complaints		☐	☐	☐

Chapter 4

General Management Techniques

What is a General Manager?

A "General Manager" is a term often used in the private sector, and refers to a generic senior manager who can manage any organisation in any sector because he or she possess excellent management skills and personal qualities. The sector, service and product knowledge is something that can be learned or provided by other staff members within the team.

In some areas of the public sector, the recruitment of general management at the most senior levels has occurred by engaging senior officers with a wide variety of backgrounds. This may mean their past experience is not necessarily from the public sector or related to the public service under their control.

A general manager should be proficient and very effective in the following areas:

* ❖ *Decision making*
* ❖ *Internal and External communication*
* ❖ *Human Resource management*
* ❖ *Financial management*
* ❖ *Quality management*

Each of the above areas are discussed in the following paragraphs, with consideration as to how certain management techniques can be successfully applied in a public sector setting.

Effective Decision Making

As discussed in chapter 2, decision making is one of the important attributes of a good public sector manager. All decisions are made with an element of uncertainty and risk. Clearly, the level of uncertainty and risk can vary dramatically, and that in itself can have a bearing on the decision making process. There are two principle ways of making a decision:

Logical Decision Making (LDM)

Involves considering objectives; planning; analysis; problem solving; alternatives; probabilities; information; facts and figures; until the most appropriate outcome is arrived at.

Instinctive Decision Making (IDM)

Involves relying on gut reactions; previous experiences; prior knowledge; risk appetite; and judgement; to arrive at the most appropriate outcome.

Both approaches can be used, and the most appropriate method will depend on the circumstances surrounding the decision. IDM is more likely to be used when instant decisions have to be made, however LDM should always be used whenever possible. There is a tendency, based on an individual's skills and personal qualities, to use one approach in favour of the other in the majority of cases. Some complex decisions require a mixture of the two approaches.

For complex decisions a useful decision making tool is the decision tree. This not only sets out all the facts of the problem being faced, it also helps establish a solution. Using this tool requires the manager to take a logical decision making approach.

The decision tree is a graphical representation which is made up of **decision points** (shown as boxes), the **alternative actions** that can be taken (shown as branches from the boxes), and the **events** that may occur, i.e. risk factors, (shown as circles). This technique is used most often in the private sector where the outcomes tend to be measured in terms of profits, as profit maximisation is usually the overriding objective. For the public sector, monetary outcomes can also be used. For example, measures could include levels of expenditure or savings, budget over or under spends, and so on.

An example of a decision tree is shown as follows:

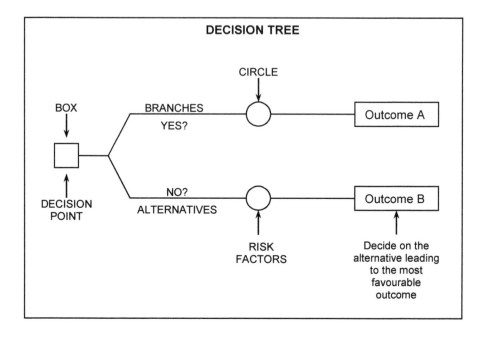

The following example uses the decision tree approach.

> **Whether to close Nursery A or Nursery B,**
> **in order to raise £1million**
> **from the sale of the building**

Closing either nursery will have an impact on the local community and the parents and children currently using the service, hence the decision will be a difficult one, but it has to be made. The service manager responsible for making the decision, has decided to take a totally logical approach by using a decision tree. The manager knows the parents of both nurseries are likely to protest, and estimates that there is a 70% probability of that happening in Nursery A and 80% probability in Nursery B.

There is a 50:50 chance that senior management will back down in the face of vigorous protest and not go ahead with the closure. In addition, although both properties have been valued at £1 million, there is only a 70% chance of Nursery A realising that amount, compared with a 90% probability that Nursery B will achieve it due to its very favourable location. With this information, the following decision tree was developed:

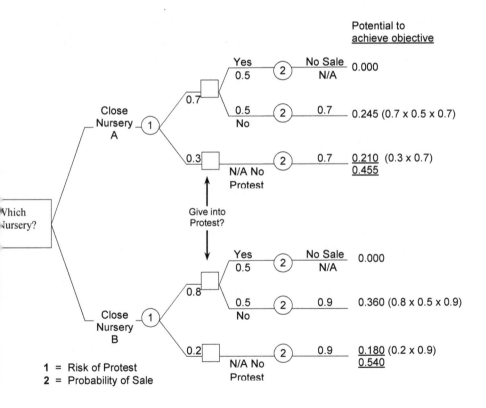

The above calculations show that using the probabilities of events around the protests and the final realisation of the £1 million, there is a greater probability of achieving the objective from closing Nursery B (0.540), than Nursery A (0.455). Hence, Nursery B should be closed and the manager can confidently demonstrate how that decision has been objectively arrived at.

The public sector manager should strive to take a LDM approach in most circumstances, although there may be occasions when the IDM approach may be the most appropriate, but these should be relatively few. It is important in the public sector that decisions can be justified and supported by facts. This is important as managers may find their decisions are questioned and scrutinised at a later date.

Effective Internal and External Communication

Managers are constantly communicating, therefore, good communication skills are one of the attributes identified in chapter 2. The key to effective communication is making sure the message is received and understood by the recipient.

Many different modes of communication can be adopted and they usually fall within the following categories:

Written: Reports, letters, notices, memos, advertisements, etc.

Verbal: Face to face, lectures, speeches, telephone, meetings, etc.

Visual: Presentations, slides, videos, television, models, photographs etc.

Audio: Recordings, radio, etc.

Electronic: E-mails, texts, websites, social networking, etc.

Many communication methods combine a mixture of two or more of the above. For example, video conferencing includes verbal, visual and audio communication.

Public sector managers will have to communicate with a wide range of people for differing purposes. These communications will include one to one discussions with individuals, raising the corporate profile through literature and public speaking, and so on. Managers regularly communicate internally and externally with the following:

Internal
- Staff
- Senior managers
- Management teams
- Boards of Directors
- Elected Members, Cabinets, Committees, Trustees

External
- Customers, users, clients, purchasers, commissioners
- General public (individuals, groups, whole community)
- Suppliers
- Contractors
- Third party stakeholders and partners

An effective communicator should ensure the correct mode of communication is used to relay the message to the target recipients.

Given that the correct mode of communication has been identified, a manager should seek to deliver the message by considering the following four stages.

STAGE 1:	Getting the receivers attention

This is the most important stage. Unless a presenter has the attention of the audience or person they wish to communicate with, the communication will fail. For example, someone making an after dinner speech will require the guests to stop talking before beginning. A manager cannot begin a staff appraisal session whilst the appraisee is concentrating on completing the appraisal form. In most instances, the receiver is expecting the message and so will initially be attentive. If the receiver is not expecting the message, getting their attention requires something more dramatic, i.e. headlines for newspaper articles, graphic billboard and advertising displays, loud hailers when speaking to demonstrators, and so on.

STAGE 2:	Maintaining the receivers attention

Having initially gained the receiver's attention, an effective communicator needs to maintain that attention throughout the duration of the communication. It is common to see audience members drifting off to sleep when listening to a boring and uninspiring presentation. Therefore, the message has to be presented to the particular individual or group in a way that would interest them. This means tailoring the style of communication, regardless of the mode used, to meet the needs of the specific receiver.

For example, a manager has plans to make a group of staff redundant and has to communicate this message to senior management, the staff being made redundant, the remaining staff, and the users that will be affected. Given the subject matter, the receivers are all likely to be initially attentive. There are two main modes of communication to be used, verbal and written. In order to ensure that the communication is effective for all the parties concerned, different styles of communication will have to be used as follows:

	Written Communication	*Verbal Communication*
Senior Management	A detailed report setting out the reason for redundancies with facts and figures, presented in tables and graphical formats to maintain interest	A presentation of the report information with visual aids if possible, allowing for questions, feedback and reflection to ensure the message has been understood
Redundant Staff	Personalised letters setting out facts and figures in an easy to understand visual format, giving details of why those staff were selected, relevant information about terms and conditions, redundancy payments, timescales, support available, and so on	Individual meetings to discuss contents of letters, dealing with concerns, giving assistance where possible, and listening to their views. The interactive and personal approach should maintain attention

	Written Communication	**Verbal Communication**
Remaining Staff	A short memoranda setting out the overall position and the reason why redundancies have been made, and the future objectives as a result of the redundancies	A group meeting where the same message is presented in a succinct manner, allowing for questions and answers to maintain interest and ensure that the message has been understood
Service Users	An official statement sent out to service users stating the position and the reasons for the decision, in a simple and brief format, with graphical presentation of relevant facts and figures, along with the impact, if any, on service delivery	A group meeting repeating the statement, but allowing for questions and answers which will ensure the message is understood and user concerns are acknowledged and dealt with

STAGE 3:	Removing the communication barriers

Even if the receiver's attention has been gained and maintained throughout the communication, the message may still not be successfully received if there are any communication barriers. These may be physical barriers such as language, sight, hearing, reading, and so on, or they may be psychological ones such as anger, fear, frustration, resentment. There are also other barriers that exist such as culture, technical jargon, time, and perceived irrelevance.

In order to remove communication barriers, the manager must first be aware that they exist. For example, if staff or users have literacy problems, communication by way of a complex report will not be understood. Similarly, if a financial training course is delivered to a group of non-financial managers using a great deal of technical jargon, the content of the communication may not be understood due to the communication barrier. A lack of understanding may lead to mis-interpretations and communication failure.

Physical barriers to communication are more easily removed than psychological ones. For example, literature can be printed in several languages, interpreters and signers can be used, subtitles can be given to videos, etc. Psychological barriers are more difficult to deal with because the manager may be less aware of their existence. For example, if a local authority is having to close a local school, it is likely that some parents may be angry and decide to demonstrate their anger by protesting. A manager, having to speak to the protestor, must understand that their anger may lead to the message not being successfully received and understood. At worst, the message may be mis-interpreted and exacerbate the existing anger.

The manager must learn about the person or group that will be receiving the communication and any potential barriers that may be present, before deciding on the mode and content of the communication.

STAGE 4:	Ensuring the message has been received and understood

This is the final stage of effective communication. It is crucial in ensuring the message has not only been heard, but has been correctly interpreted and understood in the way in which the deliverer of the message intended. There are a number of ways of confirming whether or not the message has been effectively communicated:

❖ *Asking questions of the receiver which they should be able to answer if they have understood the message*

❖ *Requesting feedback from the receiver, who should make relevant comments if they have understood the message*

❖ *Reflecting with the receiver on what has been said, i.e. they should be able to repeat the message in a way that shows understanding*

❖ *Getting the receiver to undertake an action which can only be successfully performed if the message has been properly understood*

If it is clear that the message has not been understood, the manager should

a)   establish whether or not there were any barriers to the communication and attempt to remove them

b)   consider changing the mode of communication to a form that is more appropriate (e.g. more visual images)

c)   ensure that the receiver was paying full attention in the first instance

d)   consider changing the communication style in order to maintain attention (e.g. adopting a participative rather than a lecturing style)

Repeating the message over and over again, will not necessarily achieve effective communication.

For example, a training manager asked a member of staff to produce some presentation slides in preparation for a meeting with a potential customer. When the slides were not produced the manager asked again. After the third day and the fourth request for the slides, the manager marched over to the staff member's desk only to find he was off sick with stress. The manager discussed the situation with a colleague only to discover that the staff member did not know how to use the computer to produce the requested slides. In this case, the barrier to communication was fear on the part of the staff member not wishing to be perceived as incapable. Had this barrier been removed, not only would the presentation have been produced on time (maybe by someone else), but also the staff member could have had the relevant computer training.

Effective Human Resource Management

The public sector is primarily a "service business" and therefore engages a large number of staff, who need to be managed, to deliver its services. Human resource management may be a key part of manager's role. Ideally at some point in a manager's career, they will have received training in human resource management. However, putting the theory into practice can be difficult, and staffing difficulties may have a serious impact on the ability to deliver services.

To be effective in human resource management, the manager needs to:

❖ *Be clear about the objectives to be achieved in the short and long term*

❖ *Be clear about the number and type of staff required to achieve those objectives*

❖ *Have an appropriate organisational structure to enable staff to deliver the objectives*

❖ *Have an organisational culture that gets the best out of staff*

❖ *Ensure staff are aware of how their job role contributes to the achievement of the objectives*

❖ *Have a staff training and development plan, and a programme which promotes continuous improvement in staff knowledge, skills and abilities*

❖ *Have a system of monitoring and managing staff performance against objectives*

❖ *Ensure there is an appraisal system in place*

❖ *Establish formal and informal communication systems*

❖ *Ensure appropriate personnel policies and procedures are developed, updated and implemented*

"Investors in People" (IIP) is an excellent quality standard to achieve with respect to many of the above, and provides a framework for effective human resource management. Each of the areas listed above are discussed briefly in the following paragraphs.

Clear Objectives

Every service should have clear objectives setting out what should be achieved in the short and long term. Radical change may not be necessary each year, but it is good practice to establish goals in terms of specific outcomes. Objectives should be SMART (Specific, Measurable, Achievable, Realistic, and Time Related) in nature, and easily understood by all those responsible for their achievement. For example, a police authority may have as an objective, "to reduce burglaries by 20% over the next year."

Staffing Requirements

Specifying the number and type of staff required may be relatively straight forward when beginning a new service with clear service objectives. However, difficulties may arise for an existing service where objectives may have changed but the staffing is already in place. The level and mix of staff may no longer be appropriate to meet the new objectives. This is a difficult position and may require re-organisation, re-deployment, or training and development to achieve the correct balance. There may also be an issue for some services as to whether or not to engage full time, part time or temporary staff. Services that have peaks and troughs in their work loads such as planning departments, grant giving authorities, finance departments, etc. may find that they are best suited to having a small core team and engaging temporary or contract staff as the need arise. However, too many temporary staff may result in a lack of consistency and can make human resource management more difficult. Other types of staffing requirements may include trainees, internships, sub-contractors, and secondments.

Organisational Structure

One approach to human resource management is to develop staff to the stage where they can manage themselves, or require very little management. This is achieved by "devolving" staff management to the lowest possible levels, and working towards flat management structures, therefore, avoiding situations where too many managers are managing other managers. The public sector typically has a hierarchical style of management, and tends to have more layers of management than in many private sector organisations. Not only can that lead to difficulties in communication where the wishes of senior management are slow to reach front line staff, if at all, but it is also expensive. These issues are being addressed in some sectors, but all public sector managers should consider whether or not their services are over-managed. For example, a small youth service team operating from 3 sites had a structure which included a service manager, an area manager, 3 site managers all of whom had deputies and 5 youth workers at each site; a total of 23 staff, 8 of whom had management responsibilities. In this case, the service objective of maximising the amount of contact time with young people was not being met, as too great a percentage of staff time was spent managing others.

Organisational Culture

All organisations have a culture, and in large organisations the culture may be different within each department. Culture is very important to the style of human resource management adopted, and there needs to be a cultural fit. For example, in a work culture that is very competitive in nature, staff that wish to seek recognition would tend to be keen on performance monitoring, appraisals, time recording, and so on. However, in what might be perceived to be a "blame culture", staff would tend to react negatively to these management techniques considering them to be a way of apportioning blame to individuals.

If a manager is unhappy with the existing culture, then a cultural change programme needs to be developed. This can be difficult and usually requires a lengthy timescale for implementation and achievement.

Staff Contribution to Objectives

Where the organisation has clear objectives, all staff should understand how their work contributes to achieving them. The manager should make an effort to ensure objectives are effectively disseminated, such that staff are motivated to work towards a common goal. For example, in the case of a police authority's objective to reduce burglaries, all levels of staff should be able to identify their contribution to that goal, whether it be policy makers, officers, administrators, or other support staff; a call centre passing on messages more quickly and accurately may assist in preventing or solving a burglary.

Staff Training and Development

Training and development is an important aspect of effective human resource management, and can take many forms.

Training and development not only includes qualification training and formal training courses, but also mentoring, self-development, experiential learning, supervision and so on. If training and development is really taken seriously, and time and effort applied, it can:

- *be used to improve knowledge and skills*
- *be used to increase the level of performance, productivity and quality of work*
- *enhance service quality*
- *increase staff satisfaction and motivation*
- *increase commitment*
- *change attitudes*
- *increase customer satisfaction*
- *develop effective team working*
- *assist with succession planning*

There can also be negative aspects to training and development such as increasing staff expectation beyond what the organisation can offer; improving their potential for career advancement resulting in higher staff turnover; and creating dissatisfaction as staff capabilities grow beyond their current job role. It should be stressed, the benefits that training and developing staff may bring usually far outweigh any negative aspects.

When using training and development as a management tool, it is necessary to be clear about what the service and organisation require from an individual staff member. Arising from that understanding, the organisation should then plan an appropriate programme to meet those requirements. This should be performed in conjunction with an assessment of the training requests submitted by staff. Where training requests do not fit in with the organisation's training programme, explanations should be given to staff whose requests are rejected. An annual training and development programme should be planned and implemented for all staff, based on training needs, in the acknowledgement that life long learning should lead to continuous improvement; a goal for most organisations.

Performance Monitoring and Management

Performance management techniques are a common feature in the private sector, and many public sector organisations are also introducing such systems as a means to enhance performance. In order to measure performance, each staff member needs to be set targets which they acknowledge, and are achievable. These targets should ideally be output related and quantifiable, but for some professional services this may prove difficult, in which case input and process targets can be set instead. Having set the targets, there are many techniques that can be used to assist in performance monitoring and management. These include,

- *Time sheets or work diaries*
- *Customer feedback*
- *Customer complaints*
- *Appraisals*
- *Observation*
- *Service activity statistics (e.g. numbers of visits made)*
- *Performance indicators*
- *Quality audits*
- *Team and management meetings*
- *Supervision*

- *Staff surveys and suggestions*
- *Training and assessment*
- *Flexible and multi-disciplinary working*
- *Action plans*

All the above require some form of data collection and analysis, and time for this has to be factored in when using these techniques. Ultimately the test of performance will be how well the objectives have been achieved, i.e. have the outputs, the timescales, and the budget all been met.

Appraisal Systems

This should be another essential tool for human resource management. In the private sector, appraisals are often linked to pay and benefits, and therefore seen by all staff and managers as extremely important. This means the appraisal process is prioritised by all concerned. Most appraisals undertaken by public sector organisations tend not to be linked to pay and benefits in the same way, although there are sometimes elements of performance related pay structures which are impacted by the process. The different types of appraisal system can be summarised as follows:

- *Performance appraisal where current performance, as assessed by line mangers, is measured against preset or benchmark targets*
- *Developmental appraisal where the emphasis is on current strengths and weaknesses, and training needs*
- *Upward appraisal where staff are asked to assess the performance or identify the development needs of their managers*

- *360 degree appraisals which give the appraisee feedback from a wide range of sources, including managers, peers, subordinates, customers, suppliers, and anyone who might have engaged with the appraisee in some aspect of their work, and hence can comment on performance*
- *Self appraisal where staff assess their own performance, and identify their own training needs which are then discussed with their line manager*

Some appraisals incorporate all or elements of the above systems. They are valuable to human resource management as they:

- *Provide an opportunity for discussion about individual staff performance*
- *Enable some element of performance measurement*
- *Provide an opportunity to set and monitor targets*
- *Provide an opportunity to discuss and plan training, and to gain feedback about the effectiveness and impact that training may have had*
- *Provide an opportunity to discuss how the staff member needs to contribute to the service, department, and organisational objectives*
- *Are an effective way for managers to communicate their requirements, and for staff to give feedback on a whole range of issues that may affect their performance and ability to meet those requirements*

Communication Systems

Effective internal and external communications has been discussed earlier in this chapter. Communication systems refer to the way in which communication traditionally takes place within the organisation. There will be formal and informal systems in existence such as the following:

Formal Communication Systems	Informal Communication Systems
• Organisation intranet • Regular meetings of all kinds, forums, discussion groups • Supervision sessions • Regular newsletter, magazine • Official reports, plans, memos, policies, procedures, emails • Appraisals • Training, workshops, conferences, away-days • Staff surveys, survey results • Notice boards • Official office functions	• Social networking websites • Word of mouth – grapevine • Informal networks • Unofficial groups and cliques • Emails • Coffee break chats • After work drinks, meetings, sporting activities • Unofficial functions

The manger should ensure that all the formal communication systems are working effectively. Where possible, they should also be aware of the informal communications, and any important issues arising from them.

Personnel Policies and Procedures

Human resource management requires a structure, and *personnel policies and procedures* provide an essential part of that structure. Public sector organisations tend to have very good policies and procedures covering a wide range of areas including:

- *Recruitment and selection*
- *Pay and benefits*
- *Trade Unions and Industrial Relations*
- *Equal opportunities*
- *Health and Safety*
- *Staff welfare*
- *Staff grievances*
- *Disciplinary*
- *Training and development*

None of the management techniques used should breach any of the organisation's existing policies and procedures. If there are techniques that would appear to be inconsistent with existing policies and procedures, the approach is to review and perhaps change them before adopting the technique. Human resource management should always strive to be seen to be fair and unbiased, and operating within the parameters of the existing policies and procedures and the law.

Effective Financial Management

Many areas of the public sector face the situation where the available financial resources cannot support the level of demand for services. In other cases, the services are well funded but do not maximise the use of those funds. In either situation, effective financial management is a necessary ingredient to ensure resources are properly utilised. Many public sector managers may have received no financial training throughout their career, and therefore consider themselves to have limitations in this very important area.

It is more and more common for financial management to form part of a manager's job description. Whether finances are "devolved", to front line managers or are controlled by senior managers, all managers should have a financial awareness as their actions will have a financial impact on the organisation. Understanding the relationship between service delivery and finance is paramount, and a successful manager should know how to be effective in this area. Stepping stones to effective financial management are shown in the following diagram.

Stepping stones to effective financial management

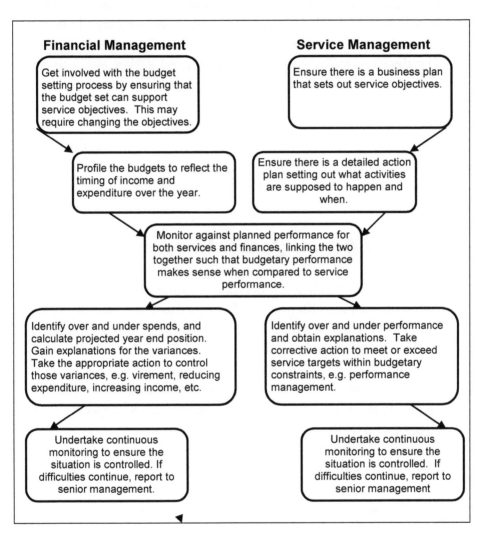

As identified above, a manager has to play an active part in financial planning, monitoring, and control, and this process should be closely linked to service management. Underpinning all the stages is the assumption that the information systems being used, provides the manager with up to date, accurate and complete information in a timely manner. If this is not the case, it may justify managers maintaining their own records in order to obtain accurate data upon which to base financial decisions. The decision making techniques discussed earlier apply to all types of decisions, particularly financial ones.

The "Essential Skills for the Public Sector" series, of which this book is a part, has a number of titles covering financial issues. Should managers require further information or development in these areas, they are highly recommended reading.

Effective Quality Management

Quality is a difficult word because it means different things to different people. Often the differences are a result of what individuals value most as opposed to cost or quantity. In the public sector, there is always a great deal of discussion about developing quality services. However, the definition of exactly what constitutes a quality service can sometimes become rather vague. It is impossible to manage quality without having first developed a quality service.

Developing a quality service

The first stage is to define what a quality service is. This may vary considerably from one service provider to another. Managers need to be clear about what quality means for their service, and this may be dictated by customers, staff, contractors, other managers, department or organisational values. In the most ideal situation everyone's definition of quality would be the same, however, this is unlikely to be the case. For example, how is quality defined for a local authority's street cleaning service?

"one that empties the bins when they are full and sweeps the streets when they need sweeping" – a local resident view

"one that meets the specification" – a contractor and management view

"one that has no variation to contract, minimises complaints and has in excess of a 90% customer satisfaction rating" – a monitoring staff view

"one that raises the profile of the local authority by ensuring the clean environment objectives are being met as far as street cleaning is concerned" – an organisational view

Hopefully all these definitions can be harmonised such that everyone is in a position to identify, whether or not the local authority's street cleaning service is a quality one.

When the quality definition has been agreed, quality standards can be set for the service. It is these quality standards that set the framework for quality monitoring, measurement and management. If a manager is to implement an effective quality management system, there must be clear quality standards in place. If this is not the case, standards must be set as the starting point of the quality management process.

When developing quality services, it may be necessary to change aspects of the organisation in order to establish the appropriate quality standards and adhere to them. This may include changing:

The organisational culture
The management style
The communication systems
The mode and style of communication
The targets and the way performance is monitored and measured

Managing the change process will require the manager to be effective in all the management techniques described in the previous paragraphs. Managing change usually requires strong leadership, decision-making, communication and motivational skills along with personal attributes such as vision, mental agility, and emotional control. Often specialist interim managers are brought in to implement the change process.

Quality Management Techniques

Quality management is very important in the light of the need to achieve value for money services. Public sector organisations should regularly review their services taking account of cost and quality. The quality aspect of the review is performed by consulting with customers, making comparisons with like organisations, benchmarking, and where relevant competing in the market place.

Quality management involves the measurement, monitoring and control of all stages of service delivery for which quality standards have been developed. Standards should have been set for the input, process, output, and the outcome of the service where this differs from the output. The quality management system should:

- *Ensure quality standards are being met in all areas of the service delivery process*
- *Identify areas which fail to meet the standards and take corrective actions*
- *Receive feedback from customers and staff on the key quality criteria for the service*
- *Continuously develop the service by reviewing standards and targets*

This process is illustrated by the following diagram.

Effective quality management techniques are summarised in the following flow chart.

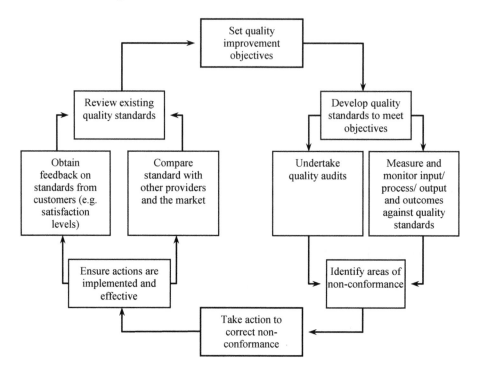

In conclusion, public sector managers should strive to develop all the general management techniques needed to face the growing challenges of:

❖ *Greater public expectations for quality*

❖ *Increasing demand for public services in some sectors*

❖ *Increased levels of scrutiny by independent monitoring bodies*

❖ *Greater devolvement of public funds*

❖ *Greater financial responsibilities for lower graded managers*

❖ *Reducing budgets for some service areas*

❖ *Increased competition from the private and the third sector in some areas*

❖ *The growing pace of organisational change*

Summary

❑ *Public sector managers need to make decisions on a regular basis. Where possible these decisions should be made in a logical way as opposed to using instinctive decision making*

❑ *Effective communication is about "getting the message across", and is best achieved by obtaining the receivers' attention, maintaining it, removing any communication barriers and ensuring that the message has been understood*

❑ *Managers often spend much of their time managing human resources. This time can be reduced if effective human resource management techniques are employed such as performance management and appraisals. In addition, good communication systems and robust policies and procedures need to be in place.*

❑ *Financial management is increasingly becoming part of a public sector manager's role. Managers need to be familiar with budget setting, monitoring variances and linking service objectives with the allocated financial resources.*

❑ *Quality issues have always been important, and even more so with the need to achieve value for money services. A public sector manager needs to develop quality services and implement quality management systems, which ensures quality is maintained and continuously improved.*

Exercise 9

Making the right decision

Listed below are a number of scenarios requiring a decision. Identify whether you would adopt logical decision making (LDM), or instinctive decision making (IDM), in each case giving your reasons

Scenario
A capital grant has been received for £450,000 and it is now month 3. It has to be spent by the end of the year, however, there are two very urgent capital projects that require financing and you have to make a choice, giving the go ahead within the next two days to either project A or B in order to ensure that the project can be completed. You personally like the sound of project A, but are not so sure about project B due to lack of knowledge. Which project do you choose?

LDM/IDM	*Reasons*

Scenario
A member of staff has lost their wallet and has asked for a loan from petty cash of £20. There is enough cash in the pettycash tin. Do you allow the loan?

LDM/IDM	*Reasons*

Scenario

You have been asked to be part of a team undertaking a review of a service in another department. This would require you undertaking a considerable amount of additional work with no allowance being made to cover your existing workload, which is already very high. Accepting membership would be greatly appreciated by the Chief Executive and the experience would, however, look good on your CV, but you are sure that your service would suffer as a result. Do you undertake the review?

LDM/IDM	*Reasons*

Scenario

You have to decide tomorrow whether or not to take advantage of a special offer on some much needed, up to date computer equipment (not essential). There is no specific budget for the purpose, but you are sure that savings can be made from another budget area to cover this small value purchase. Do you take advantage of the offer?

LDM/IDM	*Reasons*

Scenario

You are responsible for 4 hostels, one of which has to close in order to meet the target for budget reductions. Historically, they have all overspent their budgets, Hostel A being the greatest and most consistent over spender and you dislike the manager. However, occupancy rates have always been high at this hostel, whereas the others have varied considerably between sites. The decision must be made by next week.

LDM/IDM	Reasons

For suggested solutions see page 144

Exercise 10

Do you communicate effectively?

Complete the following table, and consider how you might improve the effectiveness of your internal and external communications.

Who do you communicate with	What type of messages do you try to get across	What is the most frequently used mode of communication	Are you aware of any barriers to communication	How do you ensure that your communication has been understood
Internal:				
External:				

Potential for improvement

Internal Communication:
E.g. regularity of staff meetings

External Communication:
E.g. website information

Exercise 11

How do you manage human resources?

Answer each of the following questions with either Yes or No	Yes	No
Do you have clear service objectives (SMART)?	☐	☐
Are staff aware of the objectives?	☐	☐
Do staff know how their jobs contribute to achieving the objectives?	☐	☐
Do you know how many staff you ideally require to deliver your service?	☐	☐
Do you know what mix of staff you require to delivery your service?	☐	☐
Have you achieved the correct number and mix of staff to deliver your service?	☐	☐
Is your organisational structure efficient and effective in delivering your service?	☐	☐
Is there the correct balance between managers and staff in your organisational structure?	☐	☐
Is the organisational culture performance orientated?	☐	☐
Is there a performance management system in place?	☐	☐
Are regular appraisals undertaken for all staff?	☐	☐
Are there systems in place for monitoring service output?	☐	☐
Is there a training plan for each member of staff?	☐	☐
Are staff training plans implemented each year?	☐	☐
Have you established formal communication systems with staff?	☐	☐
Are you sure that the current communication systems are effective?	☐	☐
Are you aware of all the informal communications that occur?	☐	☐

Answer each of the following questions with either Yes or No	Yes	No
Do you have a method for capturing staff suggestions?	☐	☐
Do you undertake regular staff surveys and utilise the results?	☐	☐
Are you familiar with all the personnel policies and procedures relevant to the staff under your management?	☐	☐

For answer guide see page 146

Exercise 12

Your Quality Management System

Draw a diagram of your existing quality management system, and if one does not currently exist, draw a diagram of what it should look like.

Consider whether there are any gaps in your current or proposed system that may potentially allow non-conformance to quality standards, and identify how those gaps could be filled.

Gaps/Potential Gaps: *e.g. lack of written procedures*	Solutions: *e.g. produce procedures manual*

Chapter 5

UNDERSTANDING SUPPLY AND DEMAND

Supply and Demand Curve

Supply and demand is a fundamental relationship in any economy and affects every business sector including the public sector. In the private sector, supply and demand affects the price that is charged for goods and services and the quantities produced. Understanding supply and demand becomes crucial because it will affect whether or not a sector grows, is stable, goes into decline, or disappears. When demand is strong and supply scarce there is a shortage and prices are high. This often attracts more suppliers to the market place, which changes the relationship until the supply is stronger than demand, creating a surplus, and forcing prices down until more purchasers come into the market place. This will tend to continue until an "equilibrium" is reached; a point where demand and supply becomes stable. The relationship between supply and demand is shown in the graph below:

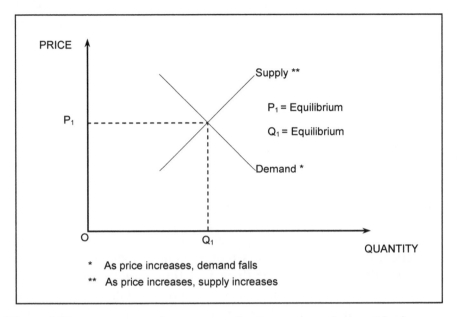

PRICE

Supply **

P_1 = Equilibrium

P_1

Q_1 = Equilibrium

Demand *

O Q_1

QUANTITY

*   As price increases, demand falls

** As price increases, supply increases

The public sector experiences exactly the same relationship in some areas. For example, Social Services departments often place children in residential care, which is mainly provided by the private and voluntary sectors. If only a few places are available at times when demand is high, the price charged per place is very high. Purchasers have little choice and have to accept the high prices. This has a direct impact on service budgets, particularly if prices increase above the budgeted levels. In contrast, if there were many available spaces and a great deal of spare capacity, the purchasers could negotiate discounts and lower prices. The impact of this may result in some homes closing down due to lack of income, and hence reducing supply again.

If public sector managers understand their market place and the factors that affect supply and demand for their services, they can make more informed strategic decisions with respect to service development, how customer needs should be met, and how financial resources should be allocated.

Factors Affecting the Supply Side

A manager should understand the "elasticity" of the supply curve for the service being provided, which is represented by the slope of the supply curve. If supply of a good or service is infinite at a particular price, then the supply curve is "perfectly elastic". Because of the elasticity the price will tend to settle at the lowest possible to produce the service, (usually cost depending on the providers requirement to make certain levels of profit). Conversely, if there is a finite supply of a good or service, the supply side will be vertical indicating that the quantities supplied will be a particular volume regardless of the prices being achieved. These are illustrated as follows:

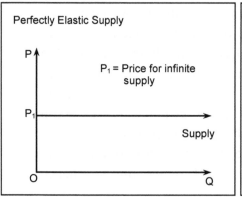

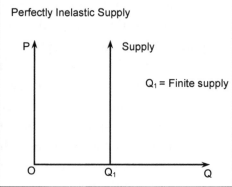

Most supply curves slope upwards from left to right and the steeper the slope the more inelastic the supply.

> For example, a hospital serving a certain catchment area has available at full capacity, a finite number of beds at any one point in time. This is an example of an inelastic supply curve and giving the hospital more money will not produce more bed spaces in the short term. It may have an impact in the longer term if the hospital builds a new hospital wing. The problem of an inelastic supply cannot necessarily be solved immediately, regardless of the available funds, (i.e. the price the community is prepared to pay).
>
> Whereas a local authority parking department will issue parking permits at a certain price to anyone eligible. This is an example of an elastic supply curve. The price stays the same regardless of short term demand, and the result can be that there are more permits issued than available spaces. In the long term, this could be corrected by increasing prices to a point that begins to affect levels of demand.

The supply side is important to the public sector, because it determines how much of a service can be supplied given the cost of supply and the available financial resources. The supply side is affected by:

❖ *Levels of demand*

(e.g. there is no point in supplying a service for which there is little or no demand to justify the cost of supply)

❖ *The price that can be achieved in relation to the cost of provision*

(e.g. for the public sector, price and cost may be the same, but if the service becomes very expensive to deliver, there

may be insufficient financial resources and the service may have to cease.)

❖ *Number of suppliers in the market place*

(e.g. if there is only one supplier, there is a monopoly situation where the supplier can control the market.

❖ *The ease at which supply can be increased or decreased*

(e.g. the availability of the right staff to deliver the service if needed – skill shortages often affect the supply side)

❖ *Barriers to entry to the market place*

(e.g. the difficulties suppliers may face when entering the market for the first time, such as high set-up costs)

Factors Affecting the Demand Side

Where a manager is responsible for purchasing goods or services for the organisation itself or for the benefit of customers, it is useful to understand the market place from the demand side. Again, a starting point is the elasticity of demand for the required goods and services. If demand for a service is finite, then it will not change regardless of the price that is set; this is perfectly inelastic demand. In such cases, making the price cheaper will not have the traditional pay off of increasing demand, i.e. demand is not price sensitive. If demand for a service is infinite, at a particular price this means that whatever volume is made available to the market, it will be consumed. This type of demand may be very price sensitive, as it might be that at a higher price there is no demand at all. This elasticity of demand is often seen with public service where the demand is very high when the service is provided for free. However, as soon as charges are introduced, the demand can significantly reduce, and in some instances totally disappear. Perfectly elastic and inelastic demand curves are illustrated as follows:

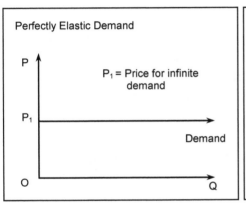

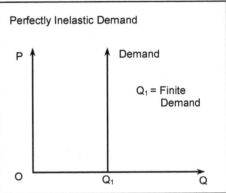

Most demand curves slope downwards from left to right and the steeper the slope the more inelastic the demand.

For example, there is usually a finite number of children of a certain age at any one point in time requiring school places. When the birth rate falls, the demand for school places reduces which may have a dramatic impact, leading to school closures due to lack of demand.

Whereas, demand for free refuse sacks delivered to households could be infinite, however when households were advised that there would be a charge of £1 for 5 sacks, the demand went to zero. This shows an infinitely elastic demand, which is very price sensitive.

The demand side is important to the public sector because it determines how much of a service needs to be supplied, and hence what level of resources need to be allocated. It also affects the way in which the public sector may wish to purchase goods and services from the market place and the price it is prepared to pay. The demand side is affected by:

❖ *Levels of supply*

(e.g. scarcity of services will result in unmet demand which may not affect price as in the private sector, but will create negative publicity and dis-satisfaction which may result in poor public relations and image.)

❖ *The price*

(e.g. the higher the price, the lower the demand depending on the elasticity)

❖ *The availability of substitutes*

(e.g. if there are a range of alternative but similar services, demand can switch from one to another)

❖ *The knowledge of what is available in the market place*

(e.g. if the purchaser does not know about other suppliers or substitutes, they may pay more for a service than is necessary)

❖ *Seasonal fluctuations leading to peaks and troughs*

(e.g. a purchaser may be able to buy outside the normal seasons and obtain better prices when demand is weak)

Market Place Imperfections

There are a number of imperfections in the market for public sector services because:

❖ *Some services are required by law and as such will have to be supplied to meet the demand regardless of price or cost*

❖ *Some services are provided whether or not demand in the normal sense exists at all, i.e. they are provided for "the common good", because society requires the service*

❖ *Some public sector market places are controlled with respect to who can supply services (e.g. approved suppliers), and who is eligible to demand certain services (e.g. criteria for free school meals)*

❖ *There are areas within the public sector where supply is finite and cannot be increased, certainly in the short term, whereas demand is infinite. This mismatch results in massive shortages at particular points in time (e.g. long social housing waiting lists which have resulted in the need to use private landlords in order to increase supply)*

In the private sector, it is common for suppliers to attempt to influence demand through advertising and promotion, pricing policies, withholding supplies to create scarcity and panic buying, reducing competition, and so on. Similarly purchasers try to influence supply by bulk purchasing to drive down prices, withholding demand causing a glut and hence price decreases, and making full use of substitution options, therefore, widening the choice of supply. In the extreme, vertical integration occurs where a company buys its main supplier to secure supply and control input prices, and horizontal integration occurs where competing suppliers merge in order to have greater control over the market place by restricting competition and controlling prices.

This pro-active involvement in the market place can also be undertaken by the public sector manager who can:

❖ *Determine levels of supply at any one point in time, restricting supply may force people to seek out substitutes. (e.g. customers turning to private health care)*

❖ *Control demand for services by setting or changing eligibility criteria*

❖ *Control prices by only contracting with suppliers who are prepared to deliver services at prescribed prices*

❖ *Undertake bulk purchasing, hence forcing down prices and controlling the supply side and avoiding shortages (e.g. block booking residential care facilities for older people)*

❖ *Merging or sharing services either across departments or even with other similar organisations. This creates economies of scale and a larger market share in terms of both supply and demand*

Public Sector Monopolies

Many public service providers find themselves in this position, certainly within a particular catchment area. Local authorities, health authorities, police authorities, and so on all have a particular area for which they provide services and some of those services are only provided by them, hence they are monopoly suppliers giving them total control of the market place subject to the nature of demand. This monopoly position means there is no competition and the supplier can exercise monopoly power in the public sector. These are a number of positive and negative aspects to public sector monopolies as follows:

Positive Aspects of Public Sector Monopoly Power	Negative Aspects of Public Sector Monopoly Power
• Can focus on quality of services and not be distracted by price competition • Can invest in research and development • If efficient, can streamline the market place and ensure services are targeted where they are most needed as opposed to where there is the most money • Can set very low prices without having to be competitive (positive for the customer) • Can decide when, where, and how much of a service should be delivered, as suits the organisation's constraints with respect to staff and finance	• Can restrict the supply of service such that demand goes unmet • Is unchallenged in the case of poor quality services due to no alternatives • Is not focused on value for money • Can end up subsidising services where no subsidy is required by the market place, (i.e. customers could afford, and would pay), leading to a poor allocation of financial resources. • Can decide when, where, and how much of a service should be delivered without reference to the demands, needs, and wants of customers

Many of the above are displayed in the way in which public services are provided. The public sector manager should be aware of whether or not they are a monopoly supplier and try not to use the monopoly power, which they have to the detriment of the user, but to develop the positive aspects that monopoly power can yield.

Summary

❑ *Public sector managers should be aware of the relationship between supply and demand in their area*

❑ *Ideally, public sector managers should be aware of the elasticity of demand and supply for services*

❑ *Given the nature of the market place, public sector managers may be able to influence the supply or the demand side for the service under their control*

❑ *In some cases it may be possible or sensible for vertical integration to take place such that the supply side can be protected*

❑ *In the case of being a monopoly service provider, care should be taken not to exploit the position by encouraging the negative aspects of a public sector monopoly*

Exercise 13

Factors affecting Supply and Demand

Consider the following types of public sector service and list what you consider to be the key factors affecting supply and demand in each area.

Residential Care for the Elderly	
Factors affecting the supply side	*Factors affecting the demand side*

Legal Services	
Factors affecting the supply side	*Factors affecting the demand side*

Ambulance Service	
Factors affecting the supply side	*Factors affecting the demand side*

The Passport Office	
Factors affecting the supply side	*Factors affecting the demand side*

For suggested solutions see page 147

Exercise 14

What is the Supply and Demand for your Service?

What type of service provider are you?
e.g. monopolist

Describe the supply side influencing factors
e.g. price

What supply side strategies do you, or should you have?
e.g. discount purchasing

Describe the demand side influencing factors
e.g. number of customers

What demand side strategies do you, or should you have?
e.g. designing eligibility criteria for customers

Chapter 6

The Public Sector Entrepreneur

Entrepreneurial Attributes

An entrepreneur is defined as *"a person who undertakes enterprise with chance of profit or loss"* The Concise Oxford Dictionary.

There are three words in this definition that do not naturally fit with the public sector, "enterprise", chance", and "profit". Most public sector services are delivered by not for profit organisations that are risk averse, and would not consider themselves an enterprise. However, entrepreneurship is apparent within the public sector, and the fact that many services now have to compete with other providers in the market place means that public sector managers sometimes need to think like, and take on the attributes of entrepreneurs.

The attributes required to be an effective public sector manager were identified in chapter 2. Ideally an entrepreneur will have the same attributes with respect to knowledge, skills and abilities as any other manager, because they will have to manage a business. However, an entrepreneur requires some additional personal qualities which are set out as follows:

Risk Taker

The entrepreneur has to balance risk and reward, usually the greater the risk the higher the potential reward. The key attribute is the ability to take calculated risks, often using probability analysis along with intuition. The ability to take risks can improve with practice after one has learnt from past mistakes.

Hard Worker

Most entrepreneurs have to work extremely hard in order to establish a business and develop it into a successful enterprise. This usually requires very long working days and working at weekends. It tends not to work well if the entrepreneur has too many other commitments elsewhere.

Visionary

The entrepreneur must have vision in order to maintain the level of commitment needed to develop a business. This is the vision of what the business will be in the future, and drives the short and long term objectives.

Creator

This does not mean that every business has to be based on a new creation, but most business try to create some kind of difference to give them a competitive advantage.

Initiator

Entrepreneurs have to be good at starting things, once the business has begun others can come in to assist in the development and realisation of the vision.

Self Starter
An entrepreneur is not someone who needs to be managed. They often have to be able to work on their own initiative without guidance and support in the first instance.

Independent
Entrepreneurs often have no choice in the early stages of their business development but to depend on themselves alone. Many entrepreneurs have to undertake every aspect of their business from strategic planning, to sales and administration.

Ambitious
Typically people choose to be entrepreneurs because they think they can be successful. This ambition for success may take many forms, it may not just be about money and profits, it may be about making a difference, recognition, innovation, being the best at something.

Confident
An enterprise is more risky than taking a job and often the rewards can be less than a salary or waged position. Hence, the entrepreneur has to be confident that they are going to succeed. This confidence should hopefully be based on something realistic and achievable which is not always the case.

Healthy
Entrepreneurship in addition to hard work, usually involves high levels of stress, particularly in relation to finances, sales, and production. It is not suited to people who suffer ill health as too much time away from the business through sickness cannot be sustained.

There are some areas of overlap with chapter 2, such as work ethic and vision, and by combining both sets of attributes it is possible to become a public sector entrepreneur.

Entrepreneurship in the Public Sector

Previous publicly owned services such as telephones, railways, gas, electricity, nuclear power and so on, are now firmly in the private sector and run as large scale enterprises with a profit maxim.

There are other areas where the public sector currently provide services that also lend themselves to entrepreneurship, because there is already an established market place:

* *Transport*
* *Legal services*
* *Finance*
* *Personnel*
* *Property management*
* *Building based centres such as leisure, halls, theatres*
* *Residential homes for the elderly, children, etc.*
* *Nursing homes*
* *Grounds maintenance*
* *Building works, repairs and maintenance*
* *Social housing provision*
* *Catering services etc. etc.*

Many public sector organisations have already put these types of services through a competitive process many of which have resulted in the private sector becoming the provider of services, and the public sector organisation being the "commissioner", (designing and specifying services) or "purchaser", (buying in the market place).

More radically, we have seen privatisation of services such as schools, prisons, and inspection services which many people would consider are not appropriate services for an enterprise culture.

Managers that currently deliver services, which could be subject to competition from the external market place, may need to be entrepreneurial themselves in order to:

- *Gain competitive advantage*
- *Keep costs at similar levels to external providers*
- *Demonstrate that they are providing value for money services*
- *Tender for services against other suppliers*
- *Manage contracts, ensuring that output levels are met and in some cases surpluses generated*

Creating an Internal Market Place

One of the first steps in creating an enterprise culture within a public sector organisation is to develop business units. This approach takes a service area and allows it to operate as a "quasi business" within the organisation but subject to a number of constraints. One such constraint may be the policy with respect to any profits made by the business unit. The business unit manager should have more autonomy to act and behave like an entrepreneur. This usually includes relaxing restrictions on purchasing, controlling bottom line budgets, and being given more freedoms with respect to human resource management.

Support services often lend themselves to this approach, and some organisations require these service areas to become self sufficient in an internal market place (where other business units, divisions and departments are customers). This approach makes these services more customer focussed as they have to win the business to survive. The only difficulty is that this type of market place is finite, with a limited number of customers, and often limited scope to really increase demand or income.

Benefits of an Entrepreneurial Approach to Public Service

There are a number of benefits which arise from the development of an enterprise culture within the public sector. These include:

❖ *Greater customer focus*

❖ *More attention to value for money*

❖ *Greater cost control*

❖ *Higher levels of productivity*

❖ *Better communication between different parts of the organisation, if an internal market exists*

❖ *Leaner management structures*

❖ *Greater creativity and innovation*

❖ *Greater flexibility in the use of resources*

❖ *Focus on generating income as opposed to spending*

❖ *Better quality control as dissatisfied customers and complaints will damage potential future custom*

It is often argued that an entrepreneurial approach is not suitable for some public sector services where priorities other than money are paramount, and a hard edged business approach does not fit well with "caring services". Entrepreneurs are often accused of:

❖ *putting finance before the service, leading to low quality and low price services that do not meet customer needs*

❖ *taking money away from direct service delivery in order to create profits*

How to Achieve More for Less

Many public services are faced with this dilemma, demand growth coupled with a reduced budget. The magical solution is "more for less" – but surely this is not possible! There are occasions where achieving more for less is within the scope of the public sector manager, particularly if an entrepreneurial approach is taken. The following factors should be considered, and if it is possible to combine one or more of the elements from the two columns simultaneously, then more for less can be achieved.

Delivering More	For Less
Increasing productivity (by reducing sickness, setting higher targets, performance management)	Reducing staff numbers
Changing the balance of staff from management to front line (flattening the organisational structure, training staff to undertake more self management, etc.)	Reducing number of managers and use part of savings for more front line staff
Greater use of technology (automating labour intensive activities, allowing customers to be more autonomous)	Use capital investment to save on revenue expenditure- buy rather than hire
New ways of delivering services (e.g. moving away from building based activities to outreach work, community based locations, shared locations, home working)	Reduce reliance on expensive offices and exchange for cheaper alternatives. Relinquish unnecessary buildings and gain capital receipts reducing debt and interest payments
Increased efficiency (reducing bureaucracy, greater accuracy, reduced wasted time and materials,)	Less paper replaced by automatic systems with in-built checks
Increased customer satisfaction (reduced complaints, reduced time spent dealing with complaints, reduced demand on resources as customers immediately satisfied, no need to come back)	Less investment in management time, meetings, review boards, and so on
Better trained workforce (more knowledge, more helpful, less waste, quicker processing, better use of IT, etc.)	Less spending on recruitment, less spending on temporary staff due to reduced sickness rates
Sharing resources or merging services with other organisations (e.g. support services such as human resource or finance departments servicing several different organisations)	Opportunities to achieve economies of scale and reduce costs, e.g. fewer senior managers required in the merged service, less accommodation required, and so on.

For example, a doctors surgery implemented a computerised repeat prescription service which allowed the receptionist to print repeat prescriptions, produce monitoring reports, flagging up patients that had asked for a certain number of repeats without going through patient's hard copy records. This enabled patients to be dealt with immediately instead of waiting to see the doctor every time. The new system resulted in reduced waiting times for all patients, higher levels of customer satisfaction, quicker and more efficient services to patients wanting repeat prescriptions and less paper work writing out repeat prescriptions, and a reduction in the need for a part time administrator as the receptionist had more time to also undertake the administrative duties. Hence, more patients were seen at a lower cost.

Delivering the Public Services of the Future

Public sector managers have to be able to change rapidly with the changing environment for public services. This means that in addition to acquiring all the attributes of a good public sector manager, they may also need to become a public sector entrepreneur, operating in a competitive environment whilst striving to maintain quality standards with a strong customer focus.

Many public services are already being delivered by private sector companies. There are a number of large corporate enterprises listed on the Stock Exchange, that have the delivery of public sector contracts as their core business and this is currently a growth area both nationally and internationally. Much of the public funding which finances the delivery of public services, is being spent in the private sector market. If public sector managers are not delivering services competitively they may be faced with the prospect of:

1. *Being absorbed within a private company taking on the delivery of the public service*

2. *Focussing on remaining in the public sector, managing third party contracts and contractors*

3. *Potentially becoming an entrepreneur and bidding to provide services themselves as a private entity*

All the above options requires the public sector manager to think more like an entrepreneur so as to ensure value for money services are delivered.

The public sector manager has to ensure that the standard of public service does not fall, but rather continues to improve in the future, regardless of who provides the service. This requires clear objectives; forward planning; strategic thinking; accurate and complete service specifications with clear service standards; and implementation of all the management techniques discussed in this book. Good luck!

Summary

❏ *Public sector managers may also need to take on some of the attributes of an entrepreneur in order to deliver public services in an entrepreneurial environment*

❏ *There are already a wide range of public services being delivered by private sector enterprises and the trend is towards the public sector scrutinising all its services for competitiveness*

❏ *Whilst there are a number of benefits of entrepreneurship within the public sector such as greater customer focus and value for money, there are reservations around reducing quality standards in order to reduce costs*

❏ *Public sector managers should not assume that it is impossible to deliver more for less without having considered every possible aspect of the way in which the service is delivered, the scope for greater productivity, and potential changes in organisational structure.*

❏ *The public sector manager of the future may need to ensure public services continue to improve and that quality is not compromised, whilst trying to achieve an entrepreneurial approach to service delivery*

Exercise 15

Do you have the personal qualities of an entrepreneur?

Answer the following questions truthfully to assess your potential for being an entrepreneur.

		Yes (✓)	No (✓)
1	Would you mortgage your house to invest in your current service	☐	☐
2	Would you mortgage your house to invest in any of the public sector service areas within your organisation	☐	☐
3	Do you work more than 10 hours of overtime each week	☐	☐
4	Do you work at weekends	☐	☐
5	Do you come up with innovative ideas for service development or improvement	☐	☐
6	Do you know what the vision is for your service area or your organisation	☐	☐
7	Do you make decisions quickly	☐	☐
8	Have you ever had any major failures which you have learned from	☐	☐
9	Are you the first one in your office most mornings	☐	☐
10	Do you manage your own workload	☐	☐

		Yes (✓)	No (✓)
11	Do you manage other people's workloads	☐	☐
12	Are you able to undertake more than one of the job roles within your service area	☐	☐
13	Do you understand all the job roles in your service area	☐	☐
14	Do you want to be Chief Executive of your organisation	☐	☐
15	Do you like working on your own	☐	☐
16	Do you prefer to work as part of a team	☐	☐
17	Do you have less than 4 days a year off as sick leave	☐	☐
18	Are you able to handle high levels of stress on a daily basis	☐	☐
19	Can you see projects through from start to finish without assistance	☐	☐
20	Do you enjoy your work	☐	☐

Unless you can answer yes to at least 80% (16) of the questions above you are perhaps best placed in a job. However, over 50% (10) yes responses show a keen entrepreneurial spirit, which is ideal for a public sector manager who may need to become a public sector entrepreneur at some time in the future.

Exercise 16

Action Plan

Given all the areas covered in this book, develop an action plan for your own personal development as a public sector manager.

Action to be taken	Training, development and learning implications	Timescale

Solutions to Exercises

Solutions to Exercises

Suggested Solution to Exercise 1
What attributes are most important?

Candidate selected
B

Reasons

The service could benefit from someone who has a lot of knowledge to compliment the fact that you are new to the service area. Also the team will benefit from someone who has strong personal qualities which hopefully coincide with your own. The lack of skills presented by the candidate can be developed with a training and development programme, and in the short term, since it is your area of strength, you can assist the new manager in areas of weakness.

If selecting a Chief Executive,
the candidate choice would be
A

Reasons

A Chief Executive requires strong personal qualities followed by good skills. The service knowledge is less important as this can be learned or provided by others in the organisation.

Answer Guide to Exercise 2
What is Your Skill Base?

Knowledge and Skills - Less than 5

Any element of knowledge or skill that attracted a score of less than 5, is an area for further development.

The nature of the development required will vary depending on the area of weakness identified. In some cases it may just require self-development action such as reading, hands on practice, copying others, etc. Other areas may benefit from more formal training sessions. It is important that a pro-active approach be taken to ensure that weak areas are strengthened, and you should identify them on the action plan provided in exercise 16. Ideally your training and development needs should be discussed during an appraisal and a training plan drawn up and implemented.

Personal Qualities - Less than 5

Scores of less than 5 in this category may be difficult to correct, but some enhancements can be made by trying to change learned habits. This may include improving your health regime, work regime, communication methods and so on. There are some techniques that can assist this process such as assertiveness training, stress management, team building, time management and so on. Peer group pressure can also have an impact in improving areas such as work ethic and general attitude.

Scores of 150 or less

Although the overall score disguises whether or not weak areas are clustered under one of the three headings discussed above, it does however suggest that there is an overall need for management development. The level of management attributes currently possessed need improvement to be a really successful public sector manager. The solution is to sign up to a comprehensive management development programme or to undertake a management diploma or degree part time. The learning points must then be put into practice if the management attributes are to really improve.

Scores between 150 and 219

As a manager you clearly have some very strong attributes, but there are also a number of weaker areas. This score shows that you are most probably viewed as a competent manager but there is clearly scope for an effective management development programme which would help you become an excellent one. It may be useful to get views from other colleagues on your attributes to ensure that you target the correct areas for improvement.

Scores of 220 and above

You have the basis for being a very good public sector manager, and the closer your score is to 280 the better you are at managing your service. Even a high score does not mean there are no weak areas that require improvement. For any area for which you scored less than 10 there is scope for further improvement. You should identify relevant self development or training opportunities wherever possible until you can reach a perfect score. You can never stop learning!

Answer Guide to Exercise 3
Is Your Manager a Good Manager?

Scores of 220 and above

You have an excellent manager who is serving you and your service area well. There may still be a few areas for further development which your manager could benefit from. When information on relevant training and development events are circulated identify them to your manager.

Scores between 150 - 219

Your manger obviously displays positive attributes in some areas but there are also areas of relative weakness that need to be addressed. As suggested above, point out learning opportunities when they arise. You could also raise concerns about the very weak areas at appraisal meetings when giving feedback about how you consider you have been managed.

Scores below 150

Your manager has perhaps been over-promoted or is new to management. It is clear that enhancement is required in a wide range of areas, some of which may improve over time or with greater experience. Encourage your manger to actively seek training and development in management skills by attending relevant courses, and raise concerns at your appraisal meetings.

Suggested Solution to Exercise 5
Developing a Customer Focus

A list of practical actions that JC could take in order to develop a more customer focussed management approach is given below.

Short Term Actions	Longer Term Actions
Open a dialogue with the prisoners on a regular basis such as holding group meetings, meeting prisoners' representatives, or setting up a discussion forum.	Implement a staff training programme covering communication skills, customer focus, prisoner welfare, quality control and so on.
Acknowledge the list of concerns and take corrective action where possible in the short term within the constraints. For points that cannot be dealt with, give reasons why.	Expand facilities or reduce the number of prisoners held at the site in order to rectify overcrowding issues.
Undertake a satisfaction survey covering a wide range of areas to establish where there is satisfaction as well as dis-satisfaction. Use the results as a benchmark for future comparisons and to measure the impact of the action plan. Hopefully satisfaction ratings will increase.	Develop or enhance current quality standards in all aspects of the service from security to prisoner welfare.
Circulate a regular bulletin or use the notice board to inform and educate prisoners about the prison process and how change can be made.	Develop a system for monitoring and reviewing the results of the action plan, along with a programme of activities for continuous improvement.

Short Term Actions	Longer Term Actions
Engage a professional counsellor or person with experience in pastoral care, and offer the service to those in need.	Prepare a written action plan that can be presented to all relevant parties and which is open to public scrutiny. This openness will hopefully create an atmosphere of trust and demonstrate a commitment to change.

Suggested Solution to Exercise 9
Making the Right Decision

Scenario	
A capital grant has been received for £450,000 and it is now month 3. It has to be spent by the end of the year, however, there are two very urgent capital projects that require financing and you have to make a choice, giving the go ahead within the next two days to either project A or B in order to ensure that the project can be completed. You personally like the sound of project A, but are not so sure about project B due to lack of knowledge.	
LDM	*Reasons* ▪ **Amount involved is large** ▪ **Importance of decision** ▪ **Cost benefit analysis could be done in time based on facts and figures**

Scenario	
A member of staff has lost their wallet and has asked for a loan from petty cash of £20. There is enough cash in the tin.	
IDM	*Reasons* ▪ **Amount involved is small** ▪ **Assumed within petty cash limits and financial regulations** ▪ **Temporary position**

Scenario

You have been asked to be part of a team undertaking a review of a service in another department. This would require you undertaking a considerable amount of additional work with no allowance being made to cover your existing workload, which is already very high. Accepting membership would be greatly appreciated by the Chief Executive and the experience would, however, look good on your CV, but you are sure that your service would suffer as a result.

	Reasons
LDM	■ **Potential impact on the existing service needs to be quantified** ■ **May need to justify the decision at a later date**

Scenario

You have to decide tomorrow whether or not to take advantage on a special offer on some much needed, up to date computer equipment (not essential). There is no specific budget for the purpose, but you are sure that savings can be made from another budget area to cover this small value purchase.

	Reasons
IDM	■ **Amount involved is small** ■ **Potential for service improvement and efficiency savings** ■ **Will satisfy current needs**

Scenario

You are responsible for 4 hostels, one of which has to close in order to meet the target for budget reductions. They have all historically overspent their budgets, Hostel A being the greatest and most consistent over spender and you dislike the manager. However, occupancy rates have always been high at this hostel, whereas the others have varied considerably between sites. The decision must be made by next week

	Reasons
LDM	■ **Impact on users and staff will need to be quantified** ■ **May need to justify the decision** ■ **Can obtain the relevant facts to make a logical decision within the time**

Answer Guide to Exercise 11
How do you Manage Human Resources?

For each yes response award 1 point and for each no response reward 0 points, then total your score.

Above 16

You have most, if not all the systems in place to ensure effective human resource management. Even though this is the case, consider whether or not the existing systems are really producing the results you require, or if there is scope for further improvement. Since communications with staff appear to be good, it may be worthwhile developing a project to review the existing systems with their input.

Between 16 and 10

There are obviously areas of good human resource management in place, but there are still areas that require development or improvement. If you really want to achieve effective human resource management you should draw up an action plan with timescales to implement change and new systems. These should then be monitored to ensure that they are achieved. Use the action plan pro-forma in exercise 16 as a tool.

Under 10

There is a lot of work to be carried out before human resource management can be considered effective in your area of service. It is likely that a fundamental change in priorities and the allocation of time and other resources needs to take place before real change and development can be implemented. The issue should be raised with senior management who may be able to assist, or the human resources (personnel) support service (if it exists), in order to get the momentum going.

Suggested Solution to Exercise 13
Factors Affecting Supply and Demand

Consider the following types of public sector services and list what you consider to be the key factors affecting supply and demand in each area.

Residential Care for the Elderly	
Factors affecting the supply side	*Factors affecting the demand side*
<ul><li>Demand for places</li><li>Quality standards to be met (barrier)</li><li>Cost of set up (barrier)</li><li>Price controls</li></ul>	<ul><li>Supply of places</li><li>Available budgets</li><li>Ageing population increasing numbers</li><li>Availability of substitute methods of care</li></ul>

Legal Services	
Factors affecting the supply side	*Factors affecting the demand side*
<ul><li>Demand</li><li>Competition</li><li>Availability of qualified staff</li></ul>	<ul><li>Price – fee rates and available budgets</li><li>Specialist areas of work reducing choice</li><li>Unpredictability of case work</li></ul>

Ambulance Services	
Factors affecting the supply side	*Factors affecting the demand side*
■ Finite number of ambulances at any one time, in any one area ■ Unpredictability of demand ■ Peaks and troughs at certain times of the day and during certain events, e.g. New Years Eve ■ Availability of qualified staff	■ Unpredictability of demand which at certain times could be infinite ■ Lack of substitutes and no competition ■ Service is "free" at point of use and so occasionally demanded when not needed ■ Lack of supply could be fatal

The Passport Office	
Factors affecting the supply side	*Factors affecting the demand side*
■ Peaks and troughs in demand affecting staffing levels ■ Monopoly supplier pros and cons, e.g. can change prices and criteria at will ■ Under public scrutiny at all times	■ Monopoly supplier pros and cons ■ Pricing policies ■ Service quality, time taken ■ Lack of substitutes and no competition ■ Service failure could have serious consequences

INDEX

A

B

C

D

E

F

G

H

I

K

L

M

N

O

P

W

Work ethic · 19, 125, 139

For further information see www.hbpublications.com
and www.fci-system.com